CHRISTIE'S
Twentieth-Century
JEWELRY

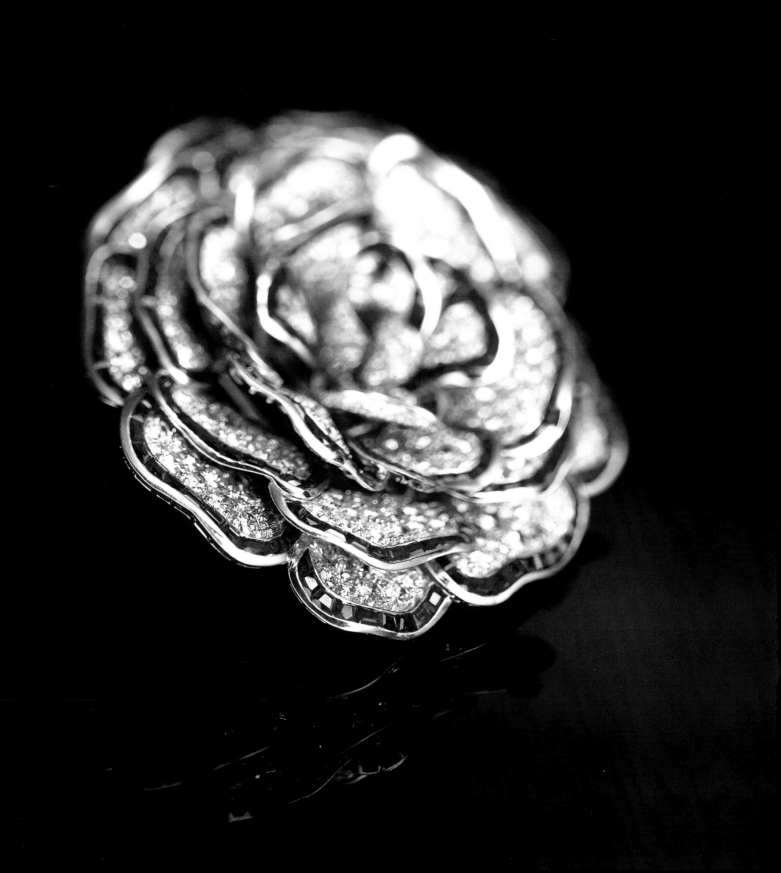

CHRISTIE'S
Twentieth-Century
JEWELRY

SALLY EVERITT AND DAVID LANCASTER

Watson-Guptill Publications
New York

First published in New York in 2002 by
Watson-Guptill Publications,
a division of VNU Business Media, Inc.,
770 Broadway, New York, NY 10003
www.watsonguptill.com

First published in 2002 in Great Britain by
PAVILION BOOKS LIMITED
64 Brewery Road, London N7 9NT
www.chrysalisbooks.co.uk

The moral rights of the authors have been asserted

DESIGNED BY: Balley Design Associates

Library of Congress Control Number: 2002106751

ISBN 0-8230-0640-9

Set in Berkeley
Colour origination by Alliance Graphics Ltd, England
Printed in Italy by Giunti Industrie Grafiche

1 2 3 4 5 6 7 8 9 10

Note: Gold amounts are listed as carats in Great Britain and karats in the
United States; so, nine-carat and eighteen-carat in Great Britain, for
example, are nine-karat and eighteen-karat, respectively, in the United States.

ABOUT CHRISTIE'S

The name of Christie's is identified throughout the world with art, expertise and connoisseurship.

In 1766 James Christie opened his London auction house and launched the world's first fine art auctioneers. Christie's reputation was established in its early years, when James Christie's saleroom became a fashionable gathering place for Georgian society, as well as for knowledgeable collectors and dealers. Christie offered artists the use of his auction house to exhibit their works and enjoyed the friendship of leading figures of the day such as Sir Joshua Reynolds, Thomas Chippendale and Thomas Gainsborough. Christie's conducted the greatest auctions of the eighteenth and nineteenth centuries, selling works of art that now hang in the world's great museums.

Over its long history, Christie's has grown into the world's leading auction house, offering sales in over eighty separate categories, which include all areas of the fine and decorative arts, collectables, wine, stamps, motor cars, even sunken cargo. There are hundreds of auctions throughout the year selling objects of every description and catering to collectors of every level.

Buyers and browsers alike will find that Christie's galleries offer changing exhibitions to rival any museum. Unlike most museums, however, in the salerooms you can touch each object and examine it up close.

Auctions are an exciting way to buy rare and wonderful objects from around the world. In the salerooms is a treasure trove of items, and while some works may sell for prices that cause a media frenzy, many of the items offered at Christie's are affordable to even the novice collector. Insiders know that auctions are a great place to pick up exceptional pieces for sensible prices.

Twentieth-century jewellery has become an exceptionally popular collecting subject in recent years. Not only can a piece be a wonderful historical object, but almost everyone has worn jewellery at some point in their lives and so everyone can relate to the subject, with famous pieces and collections such as the di Portanova jewels enhancing the appeal. Pieces of modern and contemporary jewellery have now become serious collectables, and Christie's sells twentieth-century jewellery in two auctions every year, sales that have become a highlight of many collectors' calendars.

The twentieth century presented us with a huge array of beautiful jewels of wonderfully coloured gems and precious metals. These arose from the prospecting of new gemstones plus the introduction of new materials, processes and methods of manufacture – discoveries far greater in number than any previous century has provided, and ones that would totally change our views of jewellery conception, presentation and accessibility.

INTROD

right: *Postcards from the 1900 Paris Exposition Universelle showing the moving pavement and the palace of electricity.*

As jewellers freed themselves from established and traditional ways of serving their clientele, overlapping styles crashed into each other. They reacted to the massive alterations forced by world events, not only following changing fashions but also providing important boosts to morale, confidence and the resolve to make the best of bad times.

It is not just a tale of pretty gems and glamorous styles, it is also one of fortune, glory and triumph that will appeal to all lovers of jewellery.

The story starts in the year 1900, with the attention of the world focused on Paris as the city prepared for the opening of the "Exposition Universelle". It was to be an exhibition that showcased the history, achievements and future plans of many of the countries of the world, and the banks of the River Seine were transformed by a series of specially designed pavilions in a variety of ethnic styles. The explosion of technology that was to characterize the twentieth century was clearly indicated by the motorized trucks, the escalators and the giant telescope on display, and all were brilliantly illuminated by the electricity generated in the Palace of Electrical Machines. Tourists from around the world braved "Le Trottoir

UCTION

Roulant", the moving pavement that conveyed over nine million passengers to the exhibition's diverse displays, such as "Le Palais des Lettres" and "Sciences et Arts" on the Champ-de-Mars or the forbidding and futuristic armoured dome of the "Pavillon du Creusot", which bristled with the great guns of Schneider and Co.

Dramatic presentations abounded from the moment the visitors passed through the monumental entrance arch alight with thousands of sapphire-blue lamps, and among the most enthralling was the display by René Lalique, the

genius of Art Nouveau jewellery. Lalique's jewels glittered against a background of white watered silk beneath a grey gauze, star-studded sky alive with black velvet bats. The grille protecting the display was formed by five patinated-bronze nude female figures connected by outspread wings, hinting at the evocative and erotic jewels on display within. Of far less visual appeal, but eventually of even greater significance to the history of jewellery, was Mr Mikimoto's display of a revolutionary new process. For here he revealed how, by inducing an oyster to deposit a natural pearl coating over a nucleus that had been inserted into its mantle, he could produce a pearl. It was the beginning of the giant cultured-pearl industry.

The Exposition Universelle is now acknowledged to have epitomized Art Nouveau, a style that welcomed the new century with an outpouring of organic asymmetrical designs in all aspects of the decorative arts. It was firmly rooted in the reopening of trade with Japan, which commenced in the 1860s, and in a general admiration for Japanese design, particularly its treatment of nature and combination of asymmetry with an economy of line and subtle simplicity. Japanese techniques with organic materials, colours and shadows combined with western artistic flare and recent technology to create a new and distinctive art movement that took its name from Samuel Bing's gallery, "La Maison de l'Art Nouveau".

Various countries interpreted the new movement in different ways. In Germany Art Nouveau and Arts and Crafts came together in the style termed "Jugendstil". A conjunction of art and industry, this style developed as a result of the creation in 1907 of the Deutscher Werkbund, a teaching institution guided by Henry Van der Velde and Hermann Muthesius. They created a controlled use of the "whiplash", the strong flowing lines typical of Art Nouveau, which allowed it to be repro-duced more easily in quantity. Theodor Fahrner, working in Pforzheim, the

left: *A French* minaudière *with polychrome enamel and engraved decoration influenced by the German and Austrian movements, c. 1910.*

centre of the German jewellery industry from the late eighteenth century until around 1930, established a factory producing good-quality, inexpensive jewels. His designers included Jugendstil craftsmen like Henry Van der Velde and Georg Kleemann, and his factory served a number of international outlets, such as Liberty in London, thus making these styles available to a wide audience.

The teaching of radical design created various colonies and guilds of designers. In Austria the architects Josef Hoffmann, Otto Wagner and Josef Maria Olbrich led a group known as the "Secessionists", whose designs were based on minimalist and linear functional forms that created clean and unfussy jewels.

The American jeweller Louis Comfort Tiffany followed a very different route. Concentrating on the beauty of natural form and materials, and employing the specialist skills of the gemmologist George Frederick Kunz and the brilliant designer Paulding

Farnham, he produced an award-winning range of exotic floral designs using American materials. The role of gemmologists like Kunz, who exercised scientific studies of gems to establish their chemical composition and optical properties, had only recently risen to significance. The previous centuries had seen great confusion between red stones such as ruby, spinel and garnet, and between yellow topaz and citrine, but with the emergence of the gemmologist at the turn of the twentieth century these could now be accurately classified. The rise of gemmology also resulted in a better understanding of how cutting affected a gem's appearance, ensuring the best reflection of light or deepest saturation of colour.

The concept behind these Tiffany jewels modelled on nature owed a debt to the Arts and Crafts movement. This had developed in Britain in the second half of the nineteenth century to protest at the industrialized over-ornamentation of every surface, which was so typical of the High Victorian style. Under the influence of the art critic John Ruskin and the designer William Morris, an ideal of handcrafted quality goods for the mass

right: *This cabochon cut multi-gem necklace made by The Artificers' Guild is attributed to John Houghton Maurice Bommer, c. 1905.*

market evolved; and a number of "guilds", or associations of craftsmen, were formed in the late nineteenth century to encourage and enhance various traditional trade practices. Although eventually doomed to economic failure, these guilds of art and design did become important centres for the creation and distribution of new trends.

Such was the power and impact of Art Nouveau it is often assumed that this was the only style to be seen at the beginning of the twentieth century. However, while it was ideal for the more artistic and avant-garde, it was by no means acceptable at courts throughout

Europe and among the top ranks of conservative American society. Here diamonds still ruled, and at the turn of the century the new "Garland Style" prevailed. It was initially inspired by a change in ladies' fashions. During this period, dress styles swung away from heavy cut-velvets, satins and brocades to lighter lace, organza and pale chiffons, all adorning a curved hour-glass figure, which required figure-following, light but emphatic jewels. At the same time, recent technological developments had given manufacturing jewellers the ability to work platinum, and this strong white metal proved ideally suited to diamond mounting. It allowed gem settings to be light, and diamonds were commonly held by claws for maximum exposure. However, this, together with the rapid increase in the use of electric light rather than flickering gaslight, meant that many of the nineteenth-century diamonds looked heavy and lifeless

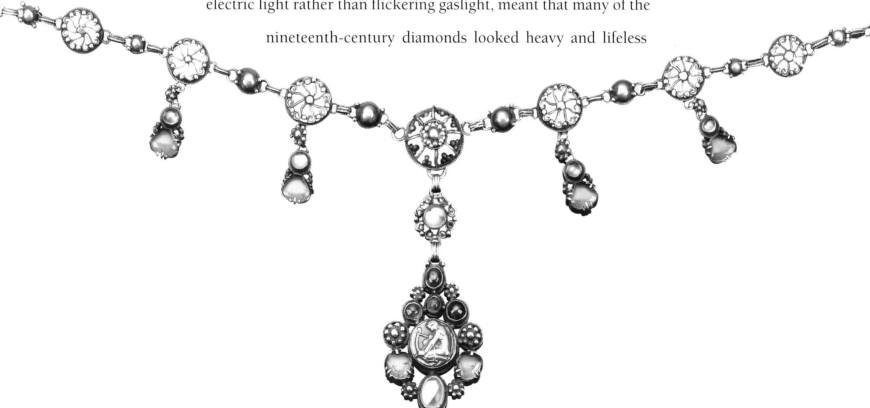

in their new settings. Consequently cutting styles changed to increase reflection at the expense of refraction, giving an overall whiter effect with fewer flashes of prismatic colour.

Following the death of Queen Victoria of Great Britain in January 1901, jewellers, and in particular the French house Cartier, were inundated with orders for new and reworked diamond jewellery in preparation for the coronation of the new king, Edward VII. Cartier subsequently opened its first London shop in New Burlington Street in 1902, and an American branch on Fifth Avenue in New York in 1909. This international expansion, which had been foretold by the international expositions of earlier years, was mirrored by other jewellers and created a more unified approach to jewellery fashion in general. The fashion leaders were the great jewellery design houses of Paris situated in the Rue de la Paix and the Place Vendôme, addresses that were to become synonymous with luxury and style, and where Cartier, Van Cleef & Arpels, Boucheron and Chaumet rubbed shoulders with the bank of the great financier J. Pierpont Morgan.

Queen Victoria's death had launched a wave of mourning jewellery in Britain, making jet, pearls and onyx the required wear as a demonstration of allegiance to the Crown, as did the death of her son, Edward VII, in 1910. The loss of the luxury liner, the *Titanic*, in 1912 saw the return of mourning jewellery on both sides of the Atlantic as huge numbers of people grieved for lost friends and relatives.

Thus the first fifteen years of the twentieth century were bedecked with a great range of jewellery, the many conflicting styles still dictated by position in the social strata. Conservative ladies clung to their multi-diamond sprays, chased and enamelled gold, mosaics and cameos, worn with the eternal diamond and gem five-stone half-hoop rings, while the fashionable sported Art Nouveau organics and members of society followed the Garland Style. These styles enjoyed a broad international acceptance, with collaboration between Cartier and Fabergé uniting Europe, Russia and the United States – a state of affairs not reflected in the politics of the day.

The war to end all wars, which began in 1914, drained the jewellery manufacturing industry of skilled craftsmen as they were called upon to manufacture armaments. There was also a much-restricted supply of materials and a dramatic decrease in the demand for the finished goods. Jewellery production continued, but at a restricted level. There was, however, one exception. The prolonged world war brought about a huge demand for sweetheart brooches, in the form of

left: *A Royal Horse Guards diamond and enamel sweetheart brooch, c. 1915, with GR monogram for Britain's King George V.*

armed forces badges and mementos in every conceivable material. Handmade trench-art cut from the brass of shell cases was conveyed home by infantrymen on leave, to be worn by their loved ones with the same pride as that displayed by officers' wives wearing the regimental badge brooches made by jewellers in diamond, gems and gold. Military-badge production was in full flow, for every able-bodied man needed to wear an indication of his reason for being home – to prove, for example, that he was on leave or injured – and patriotic symbols were also generally much in demand by the civilians left behind.

World War One brought about great changes in society, and the whole old order was turned upside down. Women's roles, in particular, underwent change. During the war many women had taken over important, formerly male-dominated, jobs while their men were away fighting and after it ended they were not keen to return to the relative obscurity and dependence of their old lives. In addition, many of them had lost their men. As they became more self-sufficient their clothing needs changed dramatically. The stiff corsets that had moulded their bodies to the earlier perceived ideal of an hour-glass figure were now discarded, and a more boyish look was adopted. Dresses were short and exposed the ankles, something that would have been totally unacceptable just a few years before; there were no defining curves; and clothes generally became more practical and very much more comfortable to wear. Long hair, which had previously been worn piled high upon the head, now fell to the hairdresser's floor as the "bob" cut became popular and this brand new image spawned a whole range of jewels to fit the new mood and flatter the new line. Long earrings suited the new haircut; and long ropes of pearls, which had been popular in the pre-war years, continued to be in vogue, but were now joined by other less orthodox materials such as amber, onyx and quartz worn as mixed-bead waistlength necklaces or graduated beads of mixed stones.

below: *The British suffragette movement adopted the colours Green, Violet and White to symbolize their aims – "Give Votes to Women".*

The barriers that clearly defined the different social strata had been breached during and after the war, and this also had an effect on jewellery production. Many more people were now willing and able to wear jewels, and the ensuing demand for more affordable pieces led to a huge increase in the production of costume jewellery. With many officers not returning, the upper class had suffered greatly and a new powerful class evolved as a result of money made during the war – the *nouveau riche*. As those who belonged to it were perceived as having no established social standing they had to "buy" this with a show of wealth that included the display of expensive and showy jewellery at their many extravagant parties.

Men returning from the war had also changed; there was an increased appetite for life, somewhat reckless at times, which manifested itself in fast cars, travel and parties. In the 1920s the world was suddenly alive again, and music, parties, Hollywood and travel became the great stimuli. However, rather than turning to the past for inspiration, as had been the case with the popular pre-war Garland Style, people looked forward to establish new designs. It was the stark lines of the more recent Vienna Secession and Bauhaus movements that underlay the emerging new styling based on geometric lines. Colour was also

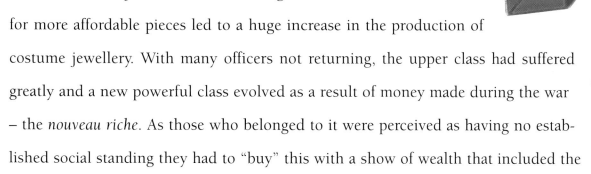

important. It was an antidote to the drabness of post-war conditions, and bright and bold gems and enamels were the theme of a Paris exhibition, "L'Exposition Internationale des Arts Décoratifs et Industriels Modernes",

above: *A fabulous set of brightly coloured, enamelled Art Deco dress clips of strong geometric design, by Chaumet, c. 1920.*

which was later to give its name to the new geometric style of this period: "Art Deco". Originally scheduled for 1916, it opened in April 1925 and displayed works of art and industry. The stated policy of the organizers was that no exhibit should imitate earlier styles and that all should display functional novelty and originality.

Compliance with these ideals encouraged and developed the pre-war design innovations, which had remained stagnant during hostilities. These incorporated the bright colours of Diaghilev's Ballets Russes as well as a strong oriental influence. Some four hundred jewellery firms took part in the exposition, and all exhibited in the Grand Palais except for one. It was Cartier who cleverly avoided this area and instead displayed his range of jewellery and accessories with the fashion houses in the Pavillon de L'Elégance, where his jewels were displayed on mannequins. The jewellery on show at the exhibition was dominated by cabochon gemstones in strong "boiled sweet" colours and stylish accessories were awarded a new importance that would last for many years to come.

Vastly improved systems of communication enabled new styles to spread rapidly on an international basis, but the jewellery industry still had its heart in Paris where the great design houses such as Cartier employed many talented artist designers. However, they usually remained anonymous behind the house signature. Creating the designs approved and accepted for Cartier by head designers Louis Cartier and Jeanne Toussaint were brilliant craftsmen such as Charles Jacqueau, Maurice Rauline, Henry Chenaud, Olivier Baloche and Gaston Vignal. Their names never appeared on finished pieces. Other designers followed a different, more independent, route. René Boivin, for instance, worked on commission for a select sophisticated clientele, spread as far afield as South America and the Middle East, who appreciated his bold and unconventional jewels. Without a showroom he travelled to meet clients including the painter Degas and the psychiatrist Sigmund Freud, and displayed his pieces at the fashion shows of his brother-in-law Paul Poiret. He was influential in popularizing the so-called "semi-precious gems" such as peridot, pink and yellow topaz, tourmaline, aquamarine, pink sapphire, cabochon-cut amethyst and moonstone. These had previously been considered inap-propriate for society jewellery, where the big five – diamond, emerald, sapphire, ruby and pearl – were the badges of wealth and privilege. Boivin also used uncon-ventional materials, making rings from dark wood set with pearls. His innovations also included the introduction in 1905 of "calibré"-cut diamonds in which the stone is cut to the shape required by the design, rather than the setting being adapted to available shapes.

above: *A 1910 Art Nouveau necklace with veined turquoise and blister pearl decoration, designed by Archibald Knox.*

This change brought about a far greater involvement of diamond cutters and lapidaries (cutters of coloured gemstones) in the design of a piece, and required close co-operation between the designer, the gem cutter, the manufacturer of the setting and the setter responsible for securing the gems in the mount to provide a finished jewel.

Around the world a pattern of fashionable showrooms, catering to the top and middle ranks of society and serviced by anonymous designers and a variety of craftsmen, was evident. In the United Kingdom, Liberty displayed the work of Archibald Knox, Jessie King, Georgina and Arthur Gaskin, and John Paul Cooper among others, without acknowledging them individually. In contrast, Peter Carl Fabergé required each of the many workmasters in his Russian workshops to include their own mark on a finished piece. Even so the workmaster would have been the head of a team of anonymous engravers, enamellers, metalworkers and setters all working together on a piece to be finished and approved by him and then possibly by Fabergé himself, before it was released to the client.

right: *Two paste set 1940s brooches by American costume jewellers Trifari, each with imitation carved sapphires, in later cases.*

This structure of intense quality control and individually crafted, labour-intensive pieces was, of course, extremely costly, and mainly produced jewels for the rich and famous. Mass production of cheaper jewellery in silver or base metal was concentrated in industrial centres such as Birmingham in England and Pforzheim in Germany, but there was also a demand for glamorous fashion jewels that were inexpensive enough to be worn a few times and then discarded. From 1910, couturiers had required flamboyant designer "faux jewels" to accessorize their costumes, and following the early lead of Paul Poiret, Coco Chanel, Schiaparelli, Premet and Driscoll

they all worked with designers to create what Chanel called "junk jewellery". The changes in society after World War One made costume jewellery more popular as many more people were willing and able to dress up; and in the United States the rise of Hollywood created a demand for this type of jewellery both as film props and to decorate the stars with a constantly changing wardrobe.

The social climate changed again quite dramatically towards the end of the 1920s, with Depression looming and fortunes being lost. In jewellery design the mood turned sombre and a more futuristic look was embraced. By the 1930s, all unnecessary ornamentation had been removed, curves were strengthened to angles and much inspiration was taken from machinery. The influences here were artist designers such as Raymond Templier (1891–1968), Gérard Sandoz (b. 1902) and Jean Dunand (1877–1942), who drew their inspiration from the defined angularity and enhanced volume of Cubism. However, as the 1930s progressed the established *haute joaillerie* of Paris rejected the dictates of economy with massive jewels of scrolls, domes, spirals, fans, bows and flowers in yellow gold set with bright-coloured gems. The dream of luxury was epitomized by the launch of the liner *Normandie* and this, plus Hollywood glamour, led to softer fashions and the creation of the luxurious – and humorous – "Cocktail Style".

World War Two saw the reintroduction of the cheaper materials of the Depression. Most of the jewels produced in this period were made in the United States from silver and paste, or semi-precious materials whose range of colours was well suited to the large flower sprays, bows and fans that were still in favour. Towards the end of the war and immediately after it, the need for humour, together with the continuing influence of Hollywood and the Disney cartoons, produced a stream of comical figural jewels, including brooches depicting clowns, ballerinas and a multitude of animals.

The 1950s returned to the glamour of the late 1930s and early 1940s, and a more feminine approach with the New Look fashions, created by Christian Dior. In jewellery, pastel colours now replaced the strong contrasts prominent in the 1920s and 1930s.

Contemporary jewellers began to emerge in significant numbers from the 1960s onwards. They produced sculptural jewels that relied on form rather than content. As well as continuing to play its traditional roles as ornament, status symbol or sentimental messenger, jewellery now developed into an art form. Innovative designs transformed the jewel into a free-standing sculpture, and new and unusual materials were introduced. One popular new material was titanium, difficult to work with but capable of providing fabulous colours. Even everyday objects were pressed into use, including woven elastic bands, paper clips and "knitted wire". During this period new cuts for gemstones were also being developed and these continued to gain popularity over the next three decades.

left & below: *A pair of butterfly brooches by JAR; the amethysts and sapphires provide a striking colour combination.*

The end of the twentieth century saw a return to glamour and romance epitomized by the marriage of Lady Diana Spencer to the Prince of Wales in the United Kingdom in 1981. However, the last decades of the century were not dominated by any one look, but characterized by an explosion of diffusely varied designs, concepts and materials that catered to a full range of tastes, uses and financial resources.

Throughout all the changes in fashion, design and materials the one feature that unites all desirable twentieth-century jewellery is exquisite workmanship. From Peter Carl Fabergé to Joel Rosenthal of JAR the ability to transform nature's materials into fabulous jewels has been maintained.

chapter one

THE BELLE ÉPOQUE

1900 to 1915

ART NOUVEAU

In 1895, Samuel Bing established La Maison de L'Art Nouveau, a gallery in Paris displaying the latest trends in the decorative arts, which was to become the keystone of, and lend its name to, an entire movement. For in this gallery Bing united the work of modern artist craftsmen from Europe, Japan and the United States, whose coming together created a new decorative style that embraced all aspects of interior design, architecture and personal ornament – Art Nouveau. Its asymmetrical organic designs, flowing abstract lines and naturalistic colours challenged the accepted decorative styles of the period, which were largely based on eighteenth-century and archaeological patterns, and represented a complete divergence from the typically cluttered ornamentation of late nineteenth-century furnishings.

The designers committed to the Art Nouveau movement produced jewellery based on nature, rendered in complex asymmetrical shapes. Nature was also reflected in their choice of materials – watery moonstones, dappled opals, peacock-feather coloured enamels and translucent horn, all reflecting an image rather than a value. This emphasis on art over worth was popular with the artistic community, including the actresses Liane de Pougy and Eleonora Duse, and with art connoisseurs proud to display the jewels as works by artists that could be worn or simply collected and appreciated. This was a very different outlook to the extravagant displays of wealth demonstrated in the diamond, gem and gold jewellery of the late nineteenth century, but the greatest challenge to established style was the introduction of sensuality. The female forms that now began to appear on jewellery in voluptuous poses were very different to the classical figures depicted in the popular Italian relief-carved agate and shell cameos of the nineteenth century. The greatest exponent of this sensual style was indubitably the French jeweller René Lalique (1860–1945). His first jewel incorporating the naked female form was a Renaissance-style cloak clasp of formal symmetrical scrolls, lines and clusters with the extraordinary addition of a nude. This was exhibited at the salon of the Société des Artistes Français at the Palais de L'Industrie, Paris, in 1895, where it was the subject of much discussion and criticism. In the same year he exhibited in Bing's gallery, alongside other designers who, like Lalique, were heavily influenced by Japanese art.

Lalique's flamboyant artistry also led him to be invited, in association with the Czech artist Alphonse Mucha, to create exotic stage jewels for the famous French actress Sarah Bernhardt, including those she wore in her roles as Iseyl and Gismonde in the plays of the same name performed at the Théâtre de la Renaissance; and it was probably Bernhardt who introduced him to Calouste Gulbenkian. Born in Scutari, Istanbul, Turkey in 1869, Gulbenkian was a pioneer in the development of

left: *An Art Nouveau enamel, diamond and pearl pendant necklace by the Belgian jewellers Wolfers, c. 1900.*

the petroleum industry in the Middle East, a skilful financier, and a connoisseur and collector of fine art. He commissioned a series of one hundred and forty-five jewels and objects from Lalique, allowing him the kind of freedom that every artist desires, to express himself without constraint. Lalique created a fabulous range of exotic jewels and works of art for Gulbenkian between 1895 and 1912, including the incredible dragonfly corsage ornament, which was one of the highlights of the 1900 Exposition Universelle in Paris (see pages 8–11). This enormous gold and enamel jewel of a metamorphic female torso, with its *plique-à-jour* (stained-glass effect) enamel and gem wings and ferocious gold claws, combines delicacy and threat, beauty and sexuality. The remarkable metamorphosis of the ferocious larval nymph to the shimmering dragonfly is combined with the sensuality and beauty of womanhood. It is an unsettling and mystic piece that continues to fascinate.

Lalique's artistry in glass, enamel, carved horn, gold and subdued numbers of precious stones can be seen in the meticulously observed plants, insects and birds that feature in his work. All are rendered with great naturalism and detail, from the touches of decay on

autumn flowers, and the diamond frosts of winter, to the exotic display of a flowering orchid. This realism, in which both the brown-edged leaf and the peacock in full display have a place, was combined with symbolism, and was echoed throughout the Art Nouveau movement. Creatures of the night, such as bats and owls, haunted forest scenes, while the iridescent colours of the peacock, butterfly and dragonfly tested the skills of enamellers to

right: *A gold and enamel brooch by René Lalique, the female form, flowers and peacock feather detail all typical of his work from this period.*

far right: *A dramatic corsage ornament by Georges Fouquet from 1901, the abalone pearl and plique-à-jour enamel fantasy fish suspending a group of baroque pearls and lapis lazuli drops from its mouth.*

the extreme. The female form continued to appear in juxtaposition with these other natural elements, often winged or floriated, and always with a sensuality that was simultaneously shocking and irresistible. Sensuality is also inherent in the slithering movement of the serpent, symbol of eternal life, which was famously transformed into a dramatic Art Nouveau bracelet for the actress Sarah Bernhardt by the French jeweller Georges Fouquet from a design by Alphonse Mucha in 1899.

Many influences came together to create the Art Nouveau style, including the discoveries of international explorers, technical advances and academic treatises. The use of plant forms in art and design was in part inspired by the proliferation of recently introduced exotic plants. These were the fruits of the specialized expeditions of the first half of the nineteenth century, and included wisteria, chrysanthemums and the rediscovered fuchsia. In 1902, Alphonse Mucha published the influential work *Documents Décoratifs*, which included jewellery designs based on plants and developed the work of Eugène Grasset, the Swiss-born architect and jewellery designer who produced the monthly publication *La Plante et Ses Applications Ornamentales* (1896 to 1900).

Books illustrated with colour prints made by the process of chromolithography, which was introduced in the 1850s, brought a new awareness of colour to a public used to black-and-white printing in all but the most expensive hand-coloured publications. Colourful posters and prints for the home spread the appreciation of art amid the rising middle class.

The writings and teaching of several influential figures of this period combined to arouse a new consciousness of the appropriate application of colour and ornament in association with form and function. In Britain these figures included the freelance designer and botanist Dr Christopher Dresser, who was an enthusiast for Japanese design and the author of *Principles of Decorative Design* (1873); the art critic and social reformer John Ruskin; and Owen Jones, whose book *The Grammar of Ornament* was published in 1856. Jones was an architect and art decorator, and superintendent of works for the 1851 Great Exhibition in London. His book illustrates ornament from the great past cultures, from the illuminated manuscripts of western Europe to Persian, Chinese and Indian sources. In it, he lays out thirty-seven propositions for the arrangement of form and colour, including the following: "beauty of form is produced by lines growing out one from the other in gradual undulations; there are no excrescences; nothing could be removed and leave the design equally good or better." These propositions influenced both Dresser and Ruskin, and contributed to the rejection of the Victorian love of ornament, which was heaped upon utilitarian items without regard to their function or line.

right: *A dragonfly and water-lily enamel pendant by Thesmar, c. 1900, showing the strong Japanese influence in Art Nouveau.*

Yet perhaps the greatest influence on the development of Art Nouveau style was the influence of Japanese art. Japan had recently been "opened up" to Europe and America with the signing of an agreement to re-open trade routes with the East in 1858. Prior to this agreement, Japan had been a closed society, visited by few Europeans and Americans and developing its own culture. The new trade between America, Europe and Japan resulted in the appearance in the west of wares in novel styles and materials, some of which were exhibited at the International Exhibition in London in 1862, and these had a huge impact on European and American design. In metalwork, the Japanese used enamels and mixed metals, combined with impressionistic style and asymmetry, to produce balanced compositions that greatly impressed the critics and became a major design source in both Europe and America. Indeed, in 1888, Samuel Bing launched an illustrated monthly journal called *Le Japon Artistique*, which was published in French, German and English, and his shops in both New York and Paris carried extensive stocks of Japanese art.

For Samuel Bing, it was a logical progression to change his Oriental Gallery in Paris into a gallery for modern art concentrating on the new Art Nouveau fashion. Although initially a brave move, by the time of the 1900 Paris Exposition Universelle (see pages 8–11), it can clearly be seen to have paid off. He had his very own pavilion at the exhibition – 'Art Nouveau Bing' – in which he showcased the work of the German-born decorative artist and designer Edward Colonna (1862–1948), the French painter and designer Georges de Feure (1868–1943), and the French designer Eugène Gaillard. However, despite enjoying great critical acclaim at the exhibition, Bing's concentration on Art Nouveau was not economically sustainable and by 1905, under the control of his son Marcel, the gallery was once again specializing in the more dependable oriental art.

René Lalique's glorious display at the 1900 Paris Exposition Universelle influenced many jewellers to turn to the new style. One such jeweller was Lucien Gaillard, who had studied Japanese techniques, and mastered the use of horn to produce hair combs of great delicacy. These combs were modelled after plants, and often adorned with shimmering moonstone

left: *A signed hair-comb by Lucien Gaillard, c. 1905, shaped and carved to depict elderberries, with cabochon sapphires and an opal.*

water droplets or inquisitive enamel bees that were extremely lifelike when viewed from afar.

Even the major French jewellery houses had to cater to the new fashion to some extent, adapting the designs to include the diamonds and pearls for which they were known and which their regular clients expected. Boucheron, for example, managed to combine fine diamonds with carved ivory to create exciting new jewels that combined the new theme of the female body with the house's trademark sprays of exotic plants, and in doing so greatly enhanced its reputation.

Although France was the centre of Art Nouveau the movement spread throughout Europe, with some designers copying the French style and others modifying it. In Germany, where Jugendstil combined the style's principles with those of the Arts and Crafts movement (see page 31), the influential designers Hermann Obrist, August Endell and Otto Eckmann sought the abstraction of organic forms – including modernistic curling tendrils combined with oddly shaped natural baroque pearls – to create modern, individual jewels. In the United States, Art Nouveau exercised a greater influence on architects such as Louis Sullivan than on jewellers, with the exception of Louis Comfort Tiffany (see pages 11–12); and although Tiffany's creations were appreciated by a handful of discerning clients, American high society clung to the glamour of diamonds and precious gems.

below: A silver and amethyst brooch by Theodor Fahrner, with maker's mark on the pin, typical of Pforzheim design.

As all these new styles took hold, demand increased and methods of mass production became involved. In the main jewellery production centre of Pforzheim, Germany, individual pieces created on commission for entrepreneurs, art lovers, society figures and the aristocracy were now being produced alongside more commercial pieces. Theodor Fahrner, for example, produced a moderately priced range of charming silver and enamel jewels, using the design expertise already in place in Pforzheim in combination with a greater degree of machine production. At the same time, however, Fahrner also continued to realize the designs of the Darmstadt colony, a consortium of individual designers allied to the British Arts and Crafts movement, including important pieces by Josef Maria Olbrich, Patriz Huber and Peter Behrens.

The Anglo-German jewellery firm of Murrle, Bennett & Co., founded in 1884 by Ernst Murrle of Pforzheim, opened a wholesale branch in London that served as a conduit to carry German Jugendstil design to Britain and British Arts and Crafts to Germany. This may explain the existence of what appear to be Archibald Knox designs with German signatures, and of German designs that carry retail markings from Liberty's of London (see page 36). Although one of the aims of the Arts and Crafts movement was to make entirely hand-produced pieces, Murrle, Bennett & Co. cleverly adapted the designs to machine production. The jewels that they produced still showed considerable individuality, combining worked surfaces with turquoise in matrix and carved opal. However, they soon faced competition in Britain from the machine-made Art Nouveau jewels produced by Charles Horner of Halifax. The Horner factory was fitted out with the latest machinery for the mass production of thimbles, hatpins and jewellery. Taking the curling line of Art Nouveau as a basic element, the jewellery was assembled in various combinations, using amethyst, citrine and enamel, to produce copies of the latest fashions for the working classes.

The commercialization and mechanization of Art Nouveau removed the freedom of line and the individuality of design that were fundamental to the very being of the movement. Determined to break away from the constant reversion to historical styles, the Art Nouveau designers of the two decades preceding and following the turn of the twentieth century had combined the glories and subtleties of nature with the finest workmanship to create beautiful individual jewels. These pieces were works of art for the discerning wealthy patron. Many, like Lalique's commissioned jewels, were never actually intended for wear, but were statements of the craft's amazing abilities. Adapting these forms to the requirements of mass production for the middle market inevitably led to stale repetitive motifs and the fashion died as quickly as it had arisen, eventually to be totally forgotten as war enveloped the world in 1914.

ARTS AND CRAFTS

In 1900, Bertha Lillian Goff, a 23-year-old student at the Holloway School of Science and Art in London, was awarded a bronze medal for her designs for a hand mirror, candlesticks, buckles and a box in the National Competition for Students of Schools of Art and Art Classes in the United Kingdom. One hundred years later, her great-niece appeared on British television's popular *Antiques Roadshow* to show the family archive of Goff's work to Geoffrey Munn, a director of specialist jewellers Wartski. Munn was intrigued and excited to find a previously unrecorded body of work that so exemplified the Arts and Crafts movement and a designer who was a true product of the schools behind the movement.

above: *A gold and pink tourmaline necklace, c. 1905, by Murrle, Bennett & Co., the back with maker's mark.*

The Arts and Crafts movement had its foundations in the realization at the Great Exhibition of 1851 in London that much of the foreign display was superior in style and ornament to the products of the British Empire. It was also a reaction to the vast increase in mechanized production during the second half of the nineteenth century. These developments drove William Morris (1834–96) – the poet, painter, craftsman and socialist writer – and others to expound the virtues of handcraft to the point of denouncing all mechanical aids to the manufacturing process, and this became the core tenet of the Arts and Crafts movement.

right: A pendant necklace by Omar Ramsden, c. 1910, the importance increased by the survival of the original case.

far right: A selection of work by Bertha Goff, illustrating her range of talents.

The movement drew its inspiration from the Middle Ages with its glorious cathedrals, splendid costumes and structured workers' guilds. Its emphasis on the individual attracted designers of the calibre of Archibald Knox, Arthur and Georgina Gaskin, C.R. Ashbee, Henry Wilson and Omar Ramsden, who delighted in being able to envision pieces valued for the love and labour of their creation rather than the intrinsic worth of the materials. Although eclipsed by the Art Nouveau movement, Arts and Crafts revealed an underlying strength and its influence was still discernible in 1930 in the studio workshops of the Scottish-born designer Sybil Dunlop. Scotland also saw the progressive adaptation of Arts and Crafts at the hands of architect and designer Charles Rennie Mackintosh of the influential Glasgow School of Art, who created a rectilinear style much admired in Austria, an important centre for modernist design, and reflected in the modern movement.

In response to the criticism of the destruction of design by industrialization voiced by Morris and John

Ruskin, the government founded a network of schools of art and design to teach the fundamentals of form and function; and the newly established South Kensington Museum in London (now the Victoria and Albert) included a gallery of bad design for reference, as well as numerous plaster casts of approved architectural styles. Bertha Goff's childhood coincided with the establishment and rise of these schools from 1880 onwards, and her natural artistic talent was well suited to the requirements of

above: An Artificers' Guild silver and gem necklace, c. 1910. The viking ship motif was used quite frequently on the Guild's pieces.

Antiques Roadshow was particularly impressed by her silver, enamel and opal pendant portraying the ancient Greek goddess of love and beauty, Aphrodite. It is a piece that displays her skill in low-relief modelling and enamelling, as well as her mastery of the handcrafting principles of Arts and Crafts. Its handworked surface finish and skilfully applied enamelling are enhanced by the natural colour-play of the opals.

Some of the pieces in this newly discovered collection are labelled and marked with prices. A beaten, silver plaque depicting the nursery rhyme shepherdess Little Bo Peep bears the label "Bertha L. Goff, 8 The Avenue, Lee, Kent, 3 guineas". However, she appears not to have signed her jewellery and thus there are undoubtedly unrecognized examples of her work on the market. Moreover, despite the price tags, it is unlikely that she would have been able to sustain herself on the proceeds of her work, and this was a common problem across the Arts and Crafts community. The movement's very insistence that every piece be entirely handcrafted ensured high costs, limited production quantities and restricted the market to commissioned items. This outcome was a far cry from William Morris' original socialist vision of the production of crafts by the artisan for the middle classes to help cure the social ills of industrialization.

Independent craftworkers like Bertha Goff who worked with limited resources could never develop a profitable market base. However, in Britain and the United States, a series of art guilds developed in the 1880s and 1890s, following in the medieval tradition, and within these communities of craftsmen the co-operative system flourished. In Britain, John Ruskin led the way with the Guild of St George, which eventually stagnated, followed by C.R. Ashbee who founded the Guild of

the Arts and Crafts ethos. She learnt her craft at the specialist art and design classes at the Holloway School, the Slade School and the Sir John Cass Technical Institute (all in London), and worked in plaster, watercolours, silver and enamel. Goff was not very well known, although she won several awards and her work was illustrated in *The Ladies Field* magazine in 1902, but she is a good example of the many independent designers encouraged by the Arts and Crafts leaders and her work reflects the kitchen handicraft style of the movement. Geoffrey Munn of

Handicraft in 1888 at Chipping Campden in Gloucester-shire, basing it firmly on socialist principles. Arthur Heygate Mackmurdo set up the Century Guild, and Nelson Dawson founded the Artificers' Guild in 1891, but the most significant and lasting of these organizations were the Art Workers' Guild (set up in 1884) and the Arts and Crafts Exhibition Society (founded in 1888), which held exhibitions triannually until World War One. Members of the Art Workers' Guild included the architects and designers John Dando Sedding and Charles F.A. Voysey; the architect, silversmith and jewellery designer C.R. Ashbee; William Morris; and the architect Edwin Lutyens.

Similar groups formed in the United States, above all the still extant Society of Arts and Crafts in Boston which was established in 1897. Twenty years later, its membership had reached one thousand under the guidance of its president Charles Eliot Norton, Professor of Fine Arts at Harvard. Norton was a friend of John Ruskin and together they developed a circle of like-minded designers and artists including William Morris, Dante Gabriel Rossetti, Edward Burne-Jones and the essayist

Thomas Carlyle. The common bond between these social reformers, Pre-Raphaelite artists and philosophers was a hatred of the effects of industrialization on art, living and working conditions and the environment. Steeped in admiration for the culture of the Middle Ages and the restorative powers of traditional country life, their goal was a return to an idealized self-sustaining lifestyle, but ultimately this could not compete with the growth of the great industrial centres.

In Austria, the architects Josef Hoffmann, Otto Wagner and Josef Maria Olbrich broke away from the Vienna Academy of Fine Art in 1897 to establish the Austrian Association of Applied Artists,

far left: *An enamelled Wiener Werkstatte brooch, c. 1910, illustrating the movement's simplistic designs, with stamped WW mark.*

below: *A buckle from the Darmstadt colony of silver plated alpaca, a copper alloy, with enamel decoration, c. 1900.*

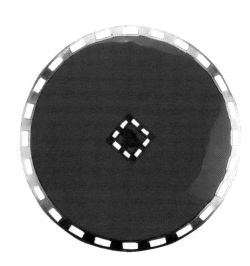

commonly known as the Secessionists. They rejected the constant reworking of historical styles, and sought to emphasize functional form with geometric angular lines and highly stylized floral motifs. In 1903, Austria also saw the development of the Wiener Werkstätte, an artists' colony dedicated to individual creativity that combined the abilities of designers, cabinetmakers, bookbinders, varnishers, goldsmiths, metalworkers, silversmiths and painters. The jewellery designers included the artist Koloman Moser, the architect Josef Hoffmann and the multitalented Dagobert Peche. This development was mirrored in Germany by the formation of the Deutsche Werkbund, which sought to unite art and industry by "the improvements of industrial producers through the collaboration of Art, Industry and Craft", under the influence of architect and designer Henry Van der Velde. Werkbund designers included Theodor Fahrner in Pforzheim, Josef Maria Olbrich and the artist colony in Darmstadt. At Darmstadt, under the patronage of Grand Duke Ernst Ludwig of Hesse, an entire town was designed by Olbrich to house the colony, attracting designers such as Hans Christiansen, Rudolph Bosselt and Patriz Huber. With the encouragement of Theodor Fahrner, they produced avant-garde jewellery embodying crisp architectural and geometrical lines combined with cabochon gems, marcasite and pearls.

In Britain, the conflict between handcrafted work and mass marketing was recognized and

below: *A polychrome enamel and silver brooch designed by Jessie M. King for Liberty, hallmarked Birmingham, 1906.*

resolved after a fashion by Arthur Lasenby Liberty, owner of Liberty's department store in Regent Street, London. His solution was to employ artist craftsmen from the guilds to design his goods, and then to mass-produce them using manufacturing techniques that simulated handcrafting. In jewellery these techniques produced items with stamped surfaces that imitated hand-finishing, but cost only a fraction of the handmade equivalent. By also refusing to acknowledge the input of the individual designers, Liberty further diluted the craft aspect. The designers he employed included Walter Crane, C.F. Voysey and Jessie M. King, who all worked in his fabric department around 1900. At the very end of the nineteenth century, he launched his Cymric and Tudric ranges of metalware including silver and enamel jewellery, buckles and buttons. These ranges were designed by eminent guild members, led by Archibald Knox, but produced by the W.H. Haseler factory in Birmingham. Knox continued to design for Liberty between 1900 and 1904, working from his home on the Isle of Man, after which time he returned to London to teach and to design for Liberty until 1912.

The American designer Louis Comfort Tiffany (1843–1933) was born into a well-established jewellery company. His own artistic talents bloomed during travels in Europe and he was inspired by oriental art and influenced by a business association with Samuel Bing and the work of René Lalique. He collaborated with Paulding Farnham on the Tiffany & Co. exhibit at the 1900 Exposition Internationale in Paris,

The Tiffany art jewellery department produced some four hundred pieces between 1902 and 1907 for exhibition and display in the main Tiffany & Co. showrooms. Louis' display at the 1904 St Louis Exposition included a gold and opal pendant in the form of a medusa jellyfish and a bronze necklace with an iridescent Favrile glass-ball fringe, and received international acclaim. Having established his individual reputation for the creation of superb jewels, particularly naturalistic floral pieces, Louis rejoined the main company of Tiffany & Co. as vice-president and they purchased the assets of Tiffany Furnaces. The output of the Tiffany Furnaces Studio was always small and exclusive, but the impact of its dramatic jewels, which freely

left: A black opal, sapphire, demantoid garnet and enamel pendant necklace by Louis Comfort Tiffany for Tiffany & Co.

combined Arts and Crafts hand-wrought workmanship with organic Art Nouveau, Byzantine and oriental motifs, established Louis Tiffany as an influential designer who ensured the highest quality in the jewels and *objets d'art* produced by the parent company.

Another exhibitor at the 1900 Exposition Internationale whose work was to have a lasting influence on the jewellery of the twentieth century was Danish ceramicist, jeweller and metalworker Georg Jensen (1866–1935). His piece "The Maid on the Jar" won an honourable mention at the exhibition, and was purchased by the Danish Museum of Decorative Art. Jensen's company employed several talented designers, including Johan Roude and Harald Nielsen, and eventually expanded to Berlin, Germany, in 1909. The Jensen blend of fruit and floral design combined Scandinavian Folk, Arts and Crafts and Art Nouveau into a distinctive house style that has withstood the test of time and is still popular today.

which included silver and enamel jewellery, buckles and buttons as well as Louis' own stained-glass windows and lamps. Two years later, back in the United States, he opened an art jewellery department at the Tiffany Furnaces Studio on 23rd Street, New York. Here he produced gold and gem hand-wrought jewellery modelled on nature, which was heavily influenced by the Arts and Crafts style. Tiffany championed American stones in his work, and under the guidance of his gemmologist, George Frederick Kunz, the public was introduced to Montana sapphire, red tourmaline from Maine and Mexican fire opal, all set in American gold. The stones were combined with gems from other countries –- lapis lazuli, turquoise, moonstone, opal and enamel. The exotic individual jewels that resulted were also clearly influenced by his earlier work on light and colour for stained-glass windows.

While the Arts and Crafts movement had its ideals firmly in the past, looking to fifteenth-century Gothic style for inspiration, its purity of line and form was reflected in the architecture of two men whose work was to have a profound impact on twentieth-century architecture: Charles Rennie Mackintosh and Frank Lloyd Wright. Mackintosh trained and taught at the Glasgow School of Art from 1890 to 1910 and Wright established an architectural practice in Chicago in 1893. Both influenced the modern movement by designing buildings that are now regarded as icons of forward thinking. Charles Rennie Mackintosh was responsible for the eclectic design of the new Glasgow School of Art in 1897, while Frank Lloyd Wright was famous for his horizontally orientated Prairie houses. Thus the influence of the Arts and Crafts movement can be seen throughout the twentieth century and spread across the world.

below left: A silver and labradorite boss design brooch by Georg Jensen, manufactured between 1908 and 1914.

THE GARLAND STYLE

The nineteenth century saw a constant scouring of history for design and had witnessed revivals of Gothic, Renaissance and Baroque styles prior to the resurgence of the Louis XVI style in the 1890s. While some early twentieth-century artist designers used Art Nouveau to escape the constant rhythm of recycled fashion, other jewellers of the first decade of the twentieth century developed the ribbon bows, floral garlands, tassels and lace motifs of the Louis XVI style, which were so beloved of courts and aristocracies, into the "Garland Style".

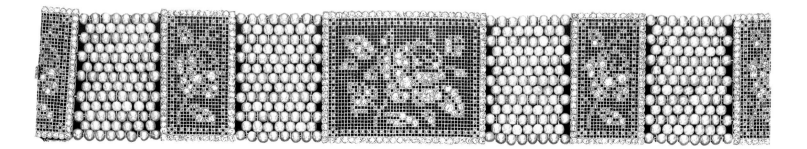

The Garland Style was enhanced by the introduction of platinum in quantity to the jeweller's workshop. This strong metal was highly suited to the creation of finely sawn and pierced trelliswork, which was delicately hinged to create light but strong flexible jewels that mimicked the flow and fall of textiles. The bright whiteness of the metal, which could be used in a nearly pure state, created an excellent background to the ever-popular diamonds. These, combined with pearls, provided just the right decoration for the pastel-coloured silks being popularized at the turn of the twentieth century by the *haute couture* of Paris. The French jewellery house Cartier responded to the new availability of platinum and the challenge of the new dress style with its range of Garland or Belle Époque jewels, using delicate wire-strung pearl trellis sections and web-pierced platinum mounts to create glittering white jewels of a distinct character.

This delicate jewellery was a vast improvement on the heavy floral styles of the late nineteenth century, which had to be mounted in substantial silver settings with gold backings to avoid tarnish marks and, due to their relative softness, were quite easily damaged. Platinum settings were very popular and so distinct from previous mounts that a flood of period jewellery was sent to the workshops for remodelling in the early years of the twentieth century. As a result, it is by no means uncommon to find a diamond bow-brooch of the first decade of the twentieth century featuring at its centre a typically nineteenth-century old-brilliant-cut diamond.

After Queen Victoria died in 1901, mourning till the last the death of her beloved consort Prince Albert forty years earlier, King Edward VII and Queen Alexandra reinstated a sense of fun in the royal court in Britain, and enjoyed a full round of pageants, balls and *fêtes champêtres*. Queen Alexandra had become an enthusiastic collector of the work of the Russian Peter Carl Fabergé (1846–1920), and for each birthday she was given a wonderful selection of his finest *objets d'art*. These gifts were put on show at court, and Fabergé's London shop soon became established as the place to purchase suitable gifts for presentation to the royal couple. Its client list embraced the entire British aristocracy and the court. The ultimate accolade for Fabergé was the commission to carve gemstone sculptures of the animals at the royal residence at Sandringham for King Edward to present to Queen Alexandra. This fashion for small precious objects achieved great popularity, and was mimicked by Tiffany, Boucheron and Cartier, who all produced *objets d'art* to grace the vitrines, or display cases, of the upper classes.

above: *This pearl and diamond bracelet by LaCloche Freres was designed to imitate* petit point *needlework, c. 1900.*

left: *A diamond and pearl bow-brooch, c. 1910. The textile ribbon design was typical of the Garland Style.*

Perhaps the most famous jewelled *objets* of the period were the gifts made by Fabergé for the Russian tsars Alexander III and Nicholas II: the imperial Easter eggs. These were produced annually from 1883 to 1915 in a great variety of styles and materials, but that of 1913 is a supreme example of the craft of the period. The egg, which is 9.5 x 6 cm (3.5 x 2.5 in), is made of a platinum network in which thousands of small square-cut coloured stones are set, creating a floral tapestry. Contained within this egg, as with nearly all of Fabergé's eggs, is a surprise – in this case a cameo of the five imperial children on a matching stand.

In the early years of the twentieth century a lady of fashion would be wearing a dress of lightly coloured silk designed by Paul Poiret or the Worth Brothers. Floral drop earrings of diamonds in flexible mounts provided flashing movement, while the neck was adorned either with a pearl or ornate diamond and pearl dog-collar choker, or a long sautoir of trellis- or rope-woven pearls with diamond and pearl twin-tassel terminals to be tied or draped as desired. A simplification of this idea was the négligé pendant necklet, perhaps so called to reflect the looseness of the gown after which it was named, where a central gem motif suspended two similar or contrasting drops at different levels to provide an asymmetric effect. Lavalliere chain necklaces terminating in asymmetric drops were also typical of the period. So too were open-work flexible bows and garlands including large stomachers and festoon corsage ornaments that covered large areas of the torso although, as the decade progressed, large sewn-on ornamentation was steadily being discarded and a scattering of several smaller lighter brooches continuing the garland theme was worn instead.

A diamond head ornament would be worn -– probably a platinum garland tiara for formal occasions, at other times an aigrette of diamonds and feathers, or a bandeau worn across the forehead. Cartier excelled in creating a range of styles for tiaras, from the "historical" to up-to-the-minute designs incorporating carved rock crystal, platinum and diamonds. In April 1911 the house staged an exhibition of nineteen tiaras worn at the coronation celebrations of King George V of Great Britain.

This was the style of the court, aristocracy and the super rich. Cartier recorded in their order books for the period 1900 to 1910 purchases by eminent figures such as Prince Alexander Bariatinsky of Russia; Queen Alexandra, the Duchess of Devonshire and Princess Victoria of Great Britain; Grand Duke Paul of Mecklenburg-Schwerin; British actress Lillie Langtry; Australian soprano Nellie Melba; the Hon. Mrs George Keppel, the last and most glamorous of the mistresses of the Prince of Wales, later Edward VII; the Brazilian pioneer aviator Alberto Santos Dumont; the American financier and industrialist Cornelius Vanderbilt; and the Aga Khan.

At the end of the first decade of the twentieth century, the all-white pearl and diamond look was modified by the introduction of black, and the popular bow-brooch now

above: *An Edwardian platinum-fronted diamond-set cluster and floral garland tiara.*

left: *A Cartier aigrette bandeau from 1913, the diamond-set tapered band with fitting to display a plume of feathers.*

featured black velvet, onyx or geometric black and white enamel. Other influences included the costumes of Diaghilev's ballet company, the Ballets Russes, particularly Paul Poiret's oriental designs for its production of *Scheherazade* in 1910. The bright colour combinations of these designs turned couturiers and jewellers alike towards the Orient for inspiration. The purity of colour and line of cabochon-cut stones (smooth domed, unfaceted gems) became very popular, and there was a new demand for the strong colours of amethyst, peridot, turquoise and fire opal in interesting combinations, while fashion began to adopt designs that incorporated vertical lines. These lines were emphasized by the cascading diamond epaulette, which in some cases continued in a sash of diamonds and pearls. This flamboyant display incorporated many design influences, including Persian, Chinese, Japanese and Indian, and ladies' turban-style headdresses, in vogue at balls around 1912, became the setting for aigrettes of diamonds and (now exotic) feathers. It was a style that echoed the court fashion of a hundred years earlier for, as publications such as the *Belle Assemblée* and *Ackermann's Repository* record, early nineteenth-century court dress for ladies had invariably included a diadem, comb or bandeau set with precious gems, which supported a magnificent

right: *A spider and web pendant necklace by Murrle, Bennett & Co., with turquoise drop and half-pearl decoration, c. 1915.*

arrangement of egret and ostrich feathers.

Pearls remained an important fashion accessory and were often worn in several ropes, ensuring that no part of the upper body was left without a covering of jewels. The popular diamond bow-brooch appeared in a range of sizes, recalling seventeenth-century fashion, the smaller ones sometimes backed with black velvet, which subsequently gave way to the black-stained agate and onyx, as styles changed from the softness of delicate materials to sterner angularity and bright polished surfaces. Similarly, tassel drops were an adaptation of eighteenth-century dress, popularized by the Ballets Russes, and developed from pearls and diamonds to the 1920 Art Deco versions in onyx, coral and pearls.

For those who could not aspire to the diamond and pearl drapes and swags of the Garland Style, and who rejected the modernism of Art Nouveau, the historicism of Arts and Crafts, and the flamboyance of the fashions inspired by the Ballets Russes, the trade continued to produce pretty jewellery, especially for the emergent middle class that was arising as a result of the spread of industrialization. Diamond or pearl crescents and stars carried over from the last century, together with the oddly popular jewelled flies, spiders and beetles, and the more predictable butterfly. Humour featured in the little monkey brooches that mothers wore, their children symbolized by demure girl monkeys sitting on a branch and naughty boy monkeys swinging below it. Hearts and pairs of hearts continued a long tradition of sentimental jewellery, as did the emblematic wings. Simple decorative effects were achieved with bar brooches, lines of variously coloured gems and diamonds. A bracelet would often be worn on each arm, delicately pierced and extensively articulated, often with a sprung or adjustable back section to ensure a snug fit – so much more practical than the stiff bangles now going out of fashion.

Wristwatches were just emerging, particularly from Cartier, with small dials surrounded by diamonds on pearl trellis bracelets. Many of the rings being worn would not look out of place today; diamond five-stone half-hoops, two-stone cross-overs and solitaires have maintained their grip on the fingers of womanhood over the last century. Here again the delicacy of platinum was exploited to produce intricate borders to the centre stones, with piercing, cross-banding and highlights in small calibré-cut coloured stones. The heart-shaped cluster with a bow surmount was also popular; sometimes the twin hearts combined a drop-cut diamond and a similarly cut coloured gem within the diamond-set border.

The significance of jewellery at the beginning of the twentieth century for all but the very poorest is well illustrated by an episode from 1906. In that year, when the magazine *Femina* offered either a pearl necklace or an automobile as prizes in a competition, seventy per cent of the contestants indicated that they would prefer the pearls. Jewellery was clearly still considered a valuable asset and a powerful social statement at this time. However, the world was about to change dramatically for all, and the luxurious lifestyle led by the upper classes was shortly to be brought to an abrupt end by the outbreak of World War One in 1914.

left: *A lady's wristwatch by Cartier, designed in 1910 and manufactured in 1920, with diamond-set bezel around the rectangular dial with platinum wire and pearl bracelet.*

SOURCING THE GEM

We can only imagine early man's first encounter with gems, but it might perhaps have been the sudden entrancing glimpse of a stone shining in the bed of a stream. It is unlikely that he would have kept hold of it in this first instance, for once dry, the stone would soon have lost its shine. Eventually man was to discover that, by rubbing their surfaces with damp sand or silt until they were smooth, stones could be made to keep their shine, and the profession of stone polisher or lapidary was established.

When the easily accessible supply of interesting stones found in riverbeds was exhausted, prospectors began to emerge. These specialists learned to track stones to their source where outcrops were being eroded by the river, and soon realized that stones were to be found in greater abundace by digging in the adjacent land.

It is known that pretty stones were valued as a trading commodity in the past. Some believe that one of Julius Caesar's reasons for invading Britain in 55 BC was to

obtain the large pearls that were to be found in British river mussels at that time. Since then nations have often gone to war over land where deposits of gold, emerald, rubies or diamonds are to be found.

The science of geology has now replaced the amateur probing of the hopeful prospector and provided an explanation of the conditions needed for nature to create gems. Pressure and heat caused by the movement of the earth can result in the formation of volcanoes or new mountain ranges, and thus the migration of certain elements that may combine to produce minerals. On rare occasions the minerals produced may be of gem quality. Carbon, which at the surface of the earth forms the soft and slippery material graphite, becomes diamond, the hardest known natural material on earth, when subjected to the heat and pressure found twenty kilometres (about twelve miles) within the earth. Furthermore, by being able to identify kimberlite, the particular rock type typical of the explosive vent that carries the diamonds towards the surface, geologists are able to map where diamond deposits might be found.

Opening a mine for gems is a high cost gamble, which involves mining, removing and processing thousands of tons of rock to produce only a tiny percentage of gem material, much of which may not be of the quality required by the jewellery industry. The few stones that do have the right

The major trading countries each have a "bourse", a specialist exchange where coloured gems or diamonds are traded by brokers, acting for the miners and cutters, to the jewellery manufacturers and designers.

An insight into the specialist trading world can be gained by attending one of the major gem and mineral fairs, such as the one held each February in Tucson, Arizona, in the United States. It is at this truly vast and totally eclectic event that many trends and themes are set or expanded upon, and the prices here often dictate worldwide costings for the jewellery industry. The fair has grown over the past twenty-five years from the original small "bring and buy" show that

colour and clarity to be classed as gems also need to be free of stress-related cracks, so that they may be safely cut and polished, and be of a shape that will yield a good sized cut gem. Many of the less important coloured stones will be cut by local industry in the mining centre, but the better quality material is passed on to specialist brokers who then sell it to experienced cutters. The cutters will carefully consider each gem, establishing its crystallography (or structure) to determine the best orientation for colour and freedom from defects. Stones may be cut to a calibrated size, an established shape and size that will fit a standard cast mount, or may be individually shaped to fit a specially made setting. Calibrated gems should also be identical in colour and brightness, so that a group set together gives a uniform effect.

1 A section through a piece of quartz, showing the varied stages of growth that finally produce the amethyst crystals.
2 A large piece of rough opal from Yowah in Australia, displaying a broad band of gem quality in the sandstone matrix.
3 A group of gem gravel from Sri Lanka, a mix of gemstones that have been dug from a river bed.

4

4 A piece of chromite rock, covered with tiny crystals of chrome-rich uvarovite garnet, forming a drusy material.

5 The optical effect in these chrysoberyl (left) and emerald (right) cat's-eye stones is caused by a series of inclusions that lie parallel to each other reflecting a band of light.

6 A late nineteenth-century brooch set with diamonds and demantoid garnets.

7 A bracelet of vari-coloured sapphires, typical of Sri Lanka.

8 The unusual electric blue of paraiba tourmaline set with diamonds to form a stunning ring.

9 This ring is set with an alexandrite, a natural form of chrysoberyl that changes colour under different lights, red in daylight and green in artificial light.

was held by the local mineral association to a massive event that attracts sellers and buyers from all over the world. Today it is a series of fairs and events spread over a two-week period that includes a variety of exhibits, from shows for trade members only and enticing stalls set up in hotel grounds to a major display that is open to the public and a great favourite with visiting school parties.

The best and most expensive gems are in the trade-only shows, although these shows also have a surprising range of prices right down to pieces for $10 or $20. Included are specialized sections for members of the jewellery and gem trade, such as the group from Idar-Oberstein, the gem-cutting centre of Europe, as well as members from G.A.N.A., the Gem Artists of North America.

Most dealers can indicate what is selling well – what colours are "in" and if there is a new variety of gemstone available. New types of fantastically coloured garnet have

appeared in the last few years, including stones that change colour in different lights. "Drusy" materials have also risen in popularity. These are gems, particularly quartz materials, that have formed as hundreds of tiny crystals on a matrix – rather like lots of coloured sparkles. These minerals are cut to shape, and can then be mounted to provide stunning effects. The paraiba tourmaline has also proved a huge recent success. These electric green and blue stones are readily available in small sizes, although it is rather more difficult to obtain stones over a couple of carats, and those that are on the market in large sizes are generally very expensive.

5

Synthetic diamonds, rubies and opals are some of the many man-made gems to be found at the Tucson fair, both as rough material and cut stones. Synthetic gems should not be confused with imitation or simulants, where an entirely different material is used to resemble another. The process used to produce these man-made variants is costly and this is reflected in the price, although prices will still be lower than those fetched by equivalent good quality natural gems.

The price of a gem is established by its rarity, desirability and of course the cost of production. Mining methods must take into consideration the nature of the stone. Hard diamond crystals will withstand rough treatment, but emeralds will break easily if not handled gently.

As old mines are exhausted, more and more exploration is conducted, and new gem sources have recently been found in Africa, Madagascar and in several of the newly independent countries that were formerly part of the Soviet Union. Political changes often have interesting results in the gem market; the bright green "demantoid" garnet, which was very popular at the beginning of the twentieth century, has suddenly reappeared after several decades of relative obscurity, as restrictions on mining and exportation were eased. New colour varieties of old established gems require a strong marketing programme to present them to the public in attractive ways. They may be draped over celebrities for example, or publicity material may stress how they are assisting fragile third world economies, anything that will lure the public away from its fixation on the traditional diamond, emerald, ruby and sapphire. There have been fears that improved synthetics may replace natural gems completely, but man's desire for beauty and rarity keeps nature on top.

chapter two

ART DECO

the 1920s and 1930s

Since the Great Exhibition in London in 1851, major gatherings of works of art and industry from around the globe have frequently served as starting points for new fashions. Following the Paris "Exposition Internationale" in 1900, which startled the world with Art Nouveau, major exhibitions in Turin in Italy in 1902 and St Louis in the United States in 1904 were notable for their displays of work by the Darmstadt colony. It is in the art work of this group that the roots of Art Deco can be found. Established in 1899 in Germany with the sponsorship of the Grand Duke Ernst Ludwig of Hesse, and inspired by the British Arts and Crafts ideal (see pages 31–8), the Darmstadt artists and designers were encouraged to freely exchange ideas and styles. The group was led by Josef Maria Olbrich, and included graphic artists and medallists Peter Behrens, Paul Bürck, Hans Christiansen, Patriz Huber, Rudolph Bosselt and Ludwig Habich. Their strong architectural-based designs emphasized a simplicity of form with minimal ornamentation, and clearly pointed the way towards the designs of Art Deco.

Further art and industry exhibitions – in London in 1908 and Brussels, Belgium, in 1910 – ensured that technology and fashion developments stayed in the news. Then, while Europe grappled with World War One, the United States continued the exhibition tradition in San Francisco in 1915 and in San Diego in 1915–16, thus allowing the European luxury trades to at least keep their names afloat. The war finally came to an end in 1918, and

Exposition des Arts Decoratifs
LA FONTAINE R LALIQUE ET LA TOUR DE BORDEAUX

Exposition des Arts Decoratifs
VUE GENERALE PRISE DES INVALIDES

above & right: *Two postcards from the Paris Exhibition of 1925, the one on the left showing the fountain designed by René Lalique.*

the exhibition that had originally been planned in Paris for 1916 opened in April 1925. It had a well-defined agenda that reflected the prevailing post-war mood of optimism. All exhibitors were required to reject the influence of the past and earlier styles and to display only items of originality. Open for six months and visited by nearly sixteen million people, the Paris "Exposition Internationale des Arts Décoratifs et Industriels Modernes" would later give its name to the style it promoted – Art Deco. It was a minimal style characterized by geometric decoration, and was to remain to a large extent centred in France, driven by the great *haute-couture* and jewellery designers of Paris, but its influence also reached further afield, as can be seen in the work of the Danish jeweller and metalworker Georg Jensen; the Belgian court jeweller Philippe Wolfers, head of Wolfers Frères; and the Italian Leopoldo Janesich, jeweller to the Duke of Aosta; all well known and influential jewellers of the time.

The jewels displayed in Paris in 1925 were highly innovative, and the methods used to promote them had also advanced. The four hundred or so jewellers exhibiting in the Grand Palais hosted the "Parure" show, inaugurated by a gala at which the French dancer, chanteuse and comedienne Mistinguett (1875–1956) appeared disguised as a "diamant solitaire", accompanied by dancers from the Paris Casino in costumes decorated with precious stones and velvet ribbons. The decision by French jeweller Louis Cartier (1875–1942) to display his jewellery in the fashion section, the Pavillon de

L'Élégance, rather than alongside the exhibits of the other jewellery houses, showed his understanding of the forces behind French designers at this time. A revolution in style was being driven by the big new names in fashion, who were now inspired by freedom from German occupation to defy convention. Always ahead of his time, in the early years of the century Cartier had already been experimenting with abstract and geometric arrangements of gems cut specifically to fit his designs, although his company was still best known for its production of the traditionally based Garland Style. He was therefore now well placed to serve a new postwar clientele enriched by the industrial and reconstruction needs of a liberated country, and swept by a desire for a faster and freer lifestyle.

The desire for freedom was immediately apparent in the new fashions in clothing for women, which followed simple lines and freed them from the corset, unwieldy hats and ground-dragging hems. Clothes became more practical and comfortable, and hemlines shorter. Coco Chanel (1883–1971) introduced new materials for women using tweeds and wools in tailored suits, while Elsa Schiaparelli (1896–1973) used an even more basic sackcloth to emphasize the new tubular line that had replaced the pre-war hour-glass shape.

above: *This emerald and diamond brooch, c. 1920 and probably by Cartier, illustrates the use of the new baguette and square cuts.*

The simplicity and freedom of these daytime clothes contrasted strongly with the very feminine evening dresses in silk and satin designed by Madame Grès (1903–93) and Madeleine Vionnet (1876–1975). These

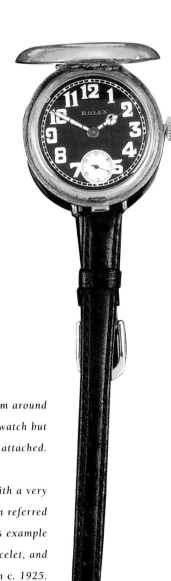

right: *An early wristwatch from around 1915, based on the pocket watch but with strap attached.*

far right: *A wristwatch with a very small rectangular dial is often referred to as the baguette type. This example has a diamond bezel and bracelet, and dates from c. 1925.*

styles emphasized the female figure and left far more of it visible and available for jewellery. Cropped hair encouraged long drop earrings, bare arms displayed several bracelets and the low-cut backs of dresses required sautoir necklaces (long chains worn loosely from the shoulders) to be as decorative from the back as from the front. The short hairstyles also gave rise to a fashion for the bandeau, a jewelled band worn across the forehead, which could often be dismantled for use as a bracelet and separate brooches. While few *bandeaux* survive today, it is probable that elements from them are still enjoyed without recognition of their previous use.

Another new accessory of growing importance was the wristwatch. This was originally developed for use by officers in the war who needed immediate access to the time without fumbling for a pocket watch, and was now a necessary adjunct to the high-speed life. All the great houses developed jewelled watches of clever and intricate design, using movements (watch mechanisms) supplied by specialists such as Léon Hatot (1883–1953). In the 1925 exposition in Paris, Hatot had been awarded a Grand Prix for his range of electrical timepieces, and in 1929 he produced the Rolls self-winding wristwatch, the world's first automatic watch. (This invention remained, however, somewhat unsung and unappreciated, appearing as it did in the middle of the havoc of the Depression.) His range of clients included the jewellers Asprey, Boucheron, Van Cleef & Arpels, Vever, Mauboussin, Janesich and Lacloche, who all retailed his watches and clocks through their expanding network of stores in Europe and the United States. His interpretation of the Art Deco style was evident in both his gem-set watch cases in geometrical shapes and his mains electric clocks that used the newly popular materials Bakelite, chrome and black

left: *An Art Deco diamond clip brooch by Cartier, in its original fitted case, c. 1930.*

enamel. Hatot's finest productions were presented to selected clients such as King Alexander of Serbia, Queen Mary of Romania, the Gaekwar of Baroda and King Faud of Egypt, and this exposure created an international market for his watches among the upper echelons of the fashion-buying world.

Always awake to new developments in the luxury market, Cartier established the European Watch and Clock Company in 1919, which created fine movements including ultra-thin and tiny versions. Cartier creativity knew no bounds, and in 1920 the firm produced a tiny diamond-set watch mounted within a pearl, as a pendant. In 1925, another pendant watch was mounted within a 136-carat emerald and purchased by one of the Dolly sisters – Rosy and Jenny were international headliners who had danced in Broadway plays and in movies. The baguette, a rectangular wristwatch shaped like the French loaf, also appeared in 1925. Cartier produced the smallest one in the world, with a width of six millimetres (about a quarter of an inch). The original baguette watch was subsequently presented to Britain's Princess (now Queen) Elizabeth by President Lebrun at the Elysée Palace during her parents' state visit to Paris in 1938.

The 1925 exposition in Paris was also the scene of an impressive display of watches from Switzerland. Having maintained their neutrality throughout the war, the

above: The simple lines of this 1930 aquamarine, rock crystal and black enamel brooch by Gustav Sandoz typify the work of the Union des Artistes Modernes.

Swiss had seized the opportunity to specialize in the manufacture of high-quality watch movements, and had built a strong industry. In 1920 alone they exported fourteen million watches and movements, then worth 306 million Swiss Francs. Prior to the war, they had specialized in producing highly decorative pocket watches for the Turkish, Abyssinian, Russian, Egyptian and Indian markets. After the war, with their industry intact and cohesive, the Swiss made full use of the 1925 exposition to launch their own range of new fashion watches throughout the world. The Omega Watch Co. of Bienne and Geneva, for example, exhibited a luxurious range. Their ladies' bracelet-watches were mostly set in platinum, decorated with diamonds, jade, ruby, sapphire, yellow sapphire, coral, emerald, onyx, lapis lazuli, Mexican fire opal, turquoise and imperial jade. While gentlemen's dress pocket-watches featured slim geometric-shaped cases, with bright cloisonné enamel within applied cells, or guilloche enamel over engine-turning, to create a play of light through the delicate enamel.

Many influences had converged in the emergence of Art Deco. It had its roots in the late nineteenth-century modernist movement that eliminated superfluous surface ornament and stressed functional simplicity. This had been founded in Germany and Austria by the painter Gustav Klimt (1862–1918) and the architects and designers Josef Hoffmann (1870–1956) and Josef Maria Olbrich (1867–1908). It was they who espoused the minimal style with geometric decoration. In Germany, the architect and designer Walter Gropius (1883–1969) founded the Bauhaus Studio to promote craftsmen designers producing prototype designs for buildings, furniture, domestic fittings and jewellery that were functional and free of excess ornament. This work influenced a new generation of artist jewellers, some of whom came together to form the Union des Artistes Modernes in France in 1929. Four jewellery designers in particular – Raymond Templier, Jean Despres, Jean Fouquet and Gérard Sandoz – concentrated on pure geometric forms, which were devoid of ornament and reflected the "machine aesthetic". Raymond Templier, for example, collaborated with the draughtsman Marcel Percheron to produce a series of Art Deco brooches of stream-lined, machine design in platinum, diamond and onyx, giving an engineered effect.

Other movements of early twentieth century Europe included Fauvism (its bright colours first exhibited in 1905 to critical disgust), Expressionism, Cubism, Futur-ism (which embraced technological progress), Neoplasticism, Constructiv-ism (the Russian equivalent of Futur-ism), Suprematism and Dadaism. Their various manifestos swept across Europe at high speed, laying the ground rules for modern design, and directly influenced the develop-ment of Art Deco in both form and colour.

News also travelled fast, and the progress of the British archaeologist and explorer Howard Carter and Lord Carnarvon at the tomb of Tutankhamun in Egypt was eagerly followed worldwide. The opening of the tomb in November 1922, and the discovery of all the wonderful pieces inside it, inspired an Egyptian revival in all aspects of life, and in jewellery in particular. Many ancient Egyptian decorative elements, from pyramids to hieroglyphics,

were incorporated into Art Deco stylized jewels that displayed the typical "boiled sweet" colours of ruby, emerald, onyx and bright enamel, and were often modelled on scarabs and temple gates. Van Cleef & Arpels, for example, produced magnificent jewellery inspired by ancient Egypt, and in particular a range of bracelets with Egyptian motifs in buff-top (domed and faceted) rubies, sapp-hires, emeralds and onyx set in a broad diamond field.

left: *The strong design of this silver, mother-of-pearl and black enamel bracelet by Victor Vasarely from around 1930 used Constructivism and optical illusion.*

The theatre also played a part in introducing new ideas of colour. The ballet company founded by Russian impresario Sergei Diaghilev (1872–1929), the Ballets Russes, introduced Russian ballet to the West when it opened for the first time in Paris in 1909 starring the dancers Pavlova, Nijinsky and Fokine. Its brilliant stage designs were by Leon Bakst, whose use of strong colour in exotic and unusual combinations inspired jewellers to incorporate such materials as red coral, blue turquoise, green amazonite, black onyx and diamond in a single flamboyant piece. *The Firebird* in 1910, *Petrushka* in 1911 and *The Rite of Spring* in 1913 established a tradition of combining music, painting, drama and dance, which energized artist designers to explore new combinations of colours and materials in brave new ways. In 1925, the African art featured in dancer

above: *A carved coral, jade and black enamel brooch by Boucheron, c. 1920, an example of the new Art Deco colours.*

below: *The Tutankhamun influence is seen in this diamond-decorated green and black enamel Egyptian revival brooch dating from the mid-1920s.*

Josephine Baker's African-American song and dance show, the *Revue Nègre*, in Paris popularized mask brooches ranging from carved Bakelite, ebony and ivory to Cartier's gold, black enamel and carved gem blackamoor heads, a fashion statement that has enjoyed frequent revivals.

The styles of other cultures were also thrown into the glorious mixture of influences behind Art Deco. The coronation of George V in Great Britain in 1911 was followed by a grand ceremony or "durbar" for him as the new Emperor of India at Delhi, at which contact between the maharajahs and Parisian designers was consolidated, resulting in a greater emphasis on Indian decorative motifs in Art Deco designs. This led, for example, to Paul Poiret including Persian-Indian aigrettes, or jewelled turban ornaments supporting sprays of exotic feathers, in his *haute-couture* designs. Also in 1911, Louis Cartier's youngest son Jacques (1884–1942) made his first journey to India with the dual result of opening the Indian market to platinum, which it eagerly embraced, and creating a craze in Europe for the polychrome enamels and colour combinations of Indian jewels. Turban-ornament designs were also modified by Cartier as hat jewels, and Indian-style tassels trailed from brooches and shoulder epaulettes. Cartier went on to establish an important export business called the Bombay Trading Co., whose agents scoured the Indian markets for fine emeralds and carved gems of typical Indian form, which were then set in suites of technicolour jewels in "giardinetto" (literally small garden) and "tutti-frutti" (fruit salad) styles. The oriental and Indo-Persian styles were also exemplified by fine jewels by Boucheron, Mellerio and Chaumet.

This was a period of experimenting with colour and cutting styles. Precious gems were mixed with onyx, coral, turquoise, jade, lapis lazuli, amber, chrysoprase and malachite, and all were carved and cut to geometric and curved shapes to provide striking colour combinations in strong outlines. The hard-stone cutting centre of Idar-Oberstein in Germany rose to prominence as demand grew for the skills of their master lapidaries, who cut, polished and sometimes set jewels. This demand was driven in part by the ever multiplying range of ladies' accessories that were now deemed necessary, partly as a result of the increased use of cosmetics in public. This

far left: *The "tutti-frutti" carved emerald and ruby flowers in this brooch, which dates from c. 1925, were inspired by Indian gems and jewels.*

left: *The panther minaudière by Cartier that reappeared seventy-five years after the design was exhibited at the 1925 Paris Exposition.*

included cigarette cases, vanity cases, lipstick holders and *minaudières*. The *minaudière* was an invention of Van Cleef & Arpels, who combined all the accessories now needed by the modern woman – powder case, cigarette case, perfume flask, lipstick, comb and mirror – in one rectangular case (or "*minaudière*") of silver and gold, set with gems and accommodated in a suede slip case in the style of an evening bag.

One of the most striking examples of the miniature artistry of Art Deco vanity cases resurfaced in a Christie's London jewellery auction in 2000. Designed by Cartier it had previously only been known from a design exhibited at the 1925 exposition in Paris. This rectangular gold case shows a black onyx panther stalking through a mother-of-pearl, onyx, turquoise and ruby landscape. The panther had become a Cartier motif from 1914 onwards, after George Barbier designed an advertising display card for the company that showed a woman in a Poiret gown with a black panther at her feet. Jeanne Toussaint – who joined Cartier at this time and was for forty years their arbiter of

fashion, combining their jewels with the designs of Elsa Schiaparelli, Christian Dior, Coco Chanel and Cristóbal Balenciaga (1895–1972) – was herself known by the pet name of "The Panther" and it was she who owned the first of Cartier's panther-decorated vanity cases, which was produced around 1917. The Cartier exhibit at the 1925 exposition was decorated with panther and zebra skins, and prowling panthers modelled in the wrought-iron balustrades. The jungle theme was a popular one in Art Deco design, and it received fresh impetus at the Colonial

Exhibition held in the grounds of the Château de Vincennes to the south-east of Paris in 1931. Included in the exhibition were jungle frescoes by Ducos de La Haille and lacquer panels of animal scenes by Jean Dunand. An example of Dunand's lacquer relief sculptures detailing Art Deco hunting scenes may be seen at the Carnegie Museum of Art in Pittsburgh, United States.

The design of accessories such as perfume bottles and compacts also rapidly developed as an art form, and these were often strikingly decorated with enamel, gems and hard-stone plaques in the Art Deco style. They sometimes incorporated nineteenth-century panels rescued from broken-up caskets, particularly ones of fine oriental carved mother-of-pearl and lacquer. Lacquer techniques were also revived in France by Indo-Chinese craftsmen, who had originally been brought to the country during the war to lacquer the wooden propeller blades of aircraft, and had stayed on in the outskirts of Paris. Lacquered goods became popular, but did not have the durability of hard-fired enamels.

Other influences on the jewellery of the 1920s and 1930s and Art Deco style came from a variety of sources, including the music scene, industry and the military. The strong influence of the Jazz Age can be seen, for example,

right: This multi-gem and diamond panel bracelet by Cartier, c. 1925, has oriental influence in the delicate flower and branch design.

below: Also dating from 1925, the strong colour combination of this jasper, enamel, turquoise and diamond bracelet by Boucheron typifies the era.

in the jewels based on the black-and-white keyboard of the piano; and the outline of a World War One tank was the inspiration for the Cartier Tank wristwatches, a design created in 1919 that remains popular to the present day.

Louis Boucheron, son of Frédéric Boucheron who founded the international jewellery company, succeeded his father as head of the firm in 1903, the year that it opened branches in New York and London. He was particularly aware of technical innovation and it was the industrial shapes of the prism, cube and trapezoid that fired his designs of innovative Art Deco jewellery for the Boucheron display at the 1925 exposition in Paris. He also popularized the bracelet-watch as an important item in a lady's wardrobe, and exhibited a large range of exciting gem-set, geometric, machine-influenced designs with matching bracelets, many with the watch face cleverly concealed. His double clip-brooches, the larger brooch dismantling to form two dress clips, rose in popularity through the late 1920s and were seized upon by fashion designer Coco Chanel. Boucheron had caught the spirit of the age with his designs, and now numbered among his clients the Maharajah of Patiala, who entrusted him with six chests of precious stones, including 1800 carats of fine emeralds, which were to be mounted in an Art Deco interpretation of traditional Indian style. The results were a hugely publicized success, and led in 1931 to an invitation by the Shah of Iran for Boucheron to catalogue

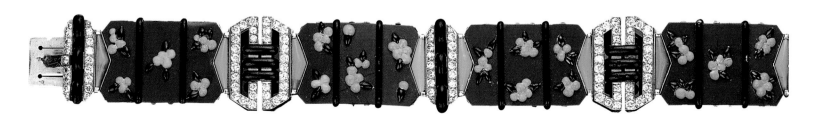

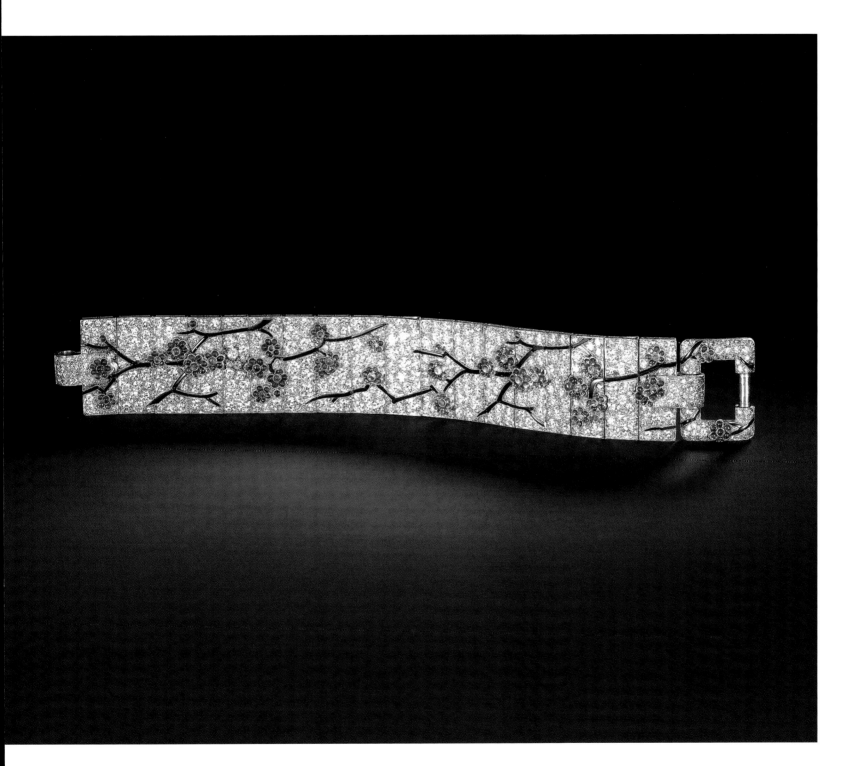

and value his treasury. Boucheron's shops in Paris, London and New York became a popular port of call for the aristocracy and wealthy families of Great Britain, the empire and the United States.

While the United States was an eager market for the new Art Deco jewellery from Paris, its own manufacturers generally remained aloof. Tiffany experimented with his own blend of varied influences and incorporated machine-age lines, particularly for precious boxes and boudoir clocks, which were also produced by Black, Starr & Frost. The most highly stylized Art Deco jewellery was produced by Marcus & Co. of New York. The Sears, Roebuck mail order catalogue featured "Moderne" jewellery in geometric shapes with faux gems made from bright-coloured paste.

above: The Art Deco black and white theme is seen here in a 1936 Cartier bangle of black lacquer, with diamond-set panel terminals that detach for use as dress clips.

THE 1930S

The Wall Street Crash in the United States in 1929, followed in the early 1930s by the worldwide economic slump, the Depression, put the brakes on the heady mix of high-speed life and high society, and had a huge impact on fashion. The American luxury market for jewellery

collapsed for a while and many small firms failed. However, the French economy was not ruined, and the showcase of wares from its African and Indo-Chinese colonies – the "Colonial Exhibition" – still went ahead in 1931, despite the gloomy world recession.

Oddly, the trend in jewellery for the emergent 1930s did not really conform with the general shift towards moderation dictated by financial strictures. The fashion in dresses became fuller and more feminine, with draped, soft materials in place of the short, straight lines of the 1920s. This was echoed by jewellery, which also softened and enlarged, into flowing ribbons, bows, sprays and plaques set throughout with diamonds, which were often pavé-set like a cobbled pavement, to create an all-white look. Thus fashion was showing its cyclical nature. Having been white and delicate before the intense colours of the 1920s it now reverted to white – but far from delicate.

Bold shapes such as the outline of the newly completed Chrysler skyscraper in New York, or the great ocean liners being promoted by Cook's Tours and popular with Americans escaping Prohibition, added new dimensions to jewellery design. Not only were the jewels large but they were worn en masse. Several chunky bracelets on each arm, pairs of dress clips, large ear clips and a bold necklace, all set throughout with diamonds in a mixture of fancy cutting styles, ensured that the wearer's social position would be recognized. Many of these jewels could be worn in different ways, necklaces separating into bracelets, earring drops detachable for day or evening wear and hook-and-eye fitting allowing pieces to be added or detached as required.

The insistence on white with only minor touches of colour led to many pieces of Victorian diamond and gold jewellery being plated with rhodium, a member of the

Telephone : WHITEHALL 2834   53-54, HAYMARKET,

SPECIALITY.

ALL COLOURED STONES CUT ON THE PREMISES.   LONDON, S.W.1. *9th June,* 1939.

M. F. C. Brown

76 Eaton Square, S.W.

JACQUES HURWITZ,

MANUFACTURING JEWELLER.   ALL ESTIMATES NETT.   DEALER IN PRECIOUS STONES.

Fine baguette and emerald brooch.   £800

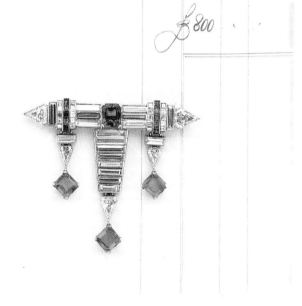

platinum family, so that they could enjoy a new lease of life. However, this was to be a short-lived trend. The jewellery displays at the 1937 "Exposition Universelle des Arts et Techniques" in Paris clearly demonstrated that the three decades of supremacy for white metals, platinum, white gold, rhodium-plated silver and nickel alloys had come to an end and yellow gold became the fashion darling again. This was used in large, sculptural areas, pavé-set with fields of diamonds so close together that almost no metal could be seen and enlivened by coloured stones or a suite of matching gems rather than the earlier colour contrasts. Big chunky bracelets and brooches with gold worked into domes, scrolls and fans pointed the way to the bold and somewhat military-influenced fashions of the 1940s.

above: *An Art Deco emerald and diamond brooch, containing various styles of cuts, accompanied by the original receipt for £800, dated 9 June 1939.*

The need to create a house style was now understood by the big jewellery houses, and each looked to their designers to create something special and distinct. In 1936, for example, Van Cleef & Arpels produced their first invisibly set brooches, using rubies and sapphires cunningly cut with a groove along the girdle that fitted into a net-like mount of platinum with no metal or gaps showing between the stones. Another characteristic Van Cleef & Arpels piece was the Ludo-Hexagone link bracelet, which was first introduced in 1934 and went on to become a hallmark of the company's production after World War Two. The design was developed under the supervision of Renée Puissant, Alfred Van Cleef's daughter and artistic director of the company from 1926 to 1942, who collaborated closely with designer René-Sim Lacaze throughout the interwar period. The best-known version of the bracelet consisted of a mosaic arrangement of articulated hexagons in polished metal, known as the beehive pattern, with a precious stone star-set at the centre of each panel. This became so popular that it was utilized in other pieces of jewellery, as well as bracelets.

below: This pair of clip brooches from 1936 combines two of Van Cleef & Arpels' special designs, the invisibly set rubies and the Ludo-Hexagone styled panels.

Boucheron followed a different path to establish a specific style for the family name. Louis Boucheron, with the aid of his sons Fred and Gerard, sent to the New York World's Fair of 1939 a range of clips in the form of intertwining feathers set with a variety of gems including moonstones, rubies, diamonds, topaz and sapphires. These proved tremendously popular with American society who loved the brightly coloured, nature-based feathers, flowers and flounces executed in bright yellow gold. Boucheron's accessories, compacts, lipstick cases, cigarette cases and lighters were also immediately recognizable by their soft and flexible, gold basket-weave outer casing. The house's name also became familiar through Yves Mirande's film *Paris–New York*, in which the suitably named Inspector Boucheron followed the trail of a stolen diamond, aboard the liner *Normandie* and to the French Pavilion at the World's Fair.

The jewellery that Boucheron and several other great French jewel houses sent to New York never returned to Paris. The opening of the fair coincided almost exactly with the declaration of World War Two. On 1 September 1939 German troops marched into Poland and for the next eight years Europe would have little call for the joy of fine jewellery.

Boucheron also employed invisible settings, which they displayed at the New York World's Fair in 1939, along with strong floral designs using cabochon rubies, citrines and moonstones. Their double clips were produced in a range of diamond scrolls and volutes, and cleverly constructed to give alternative means of joining the clips to produce varied effects. The broad expanses of gold popular at the end of the decade became in Boucheron's hands wonderful flowing scrolls reminiscent of basket weave on a grand scale.

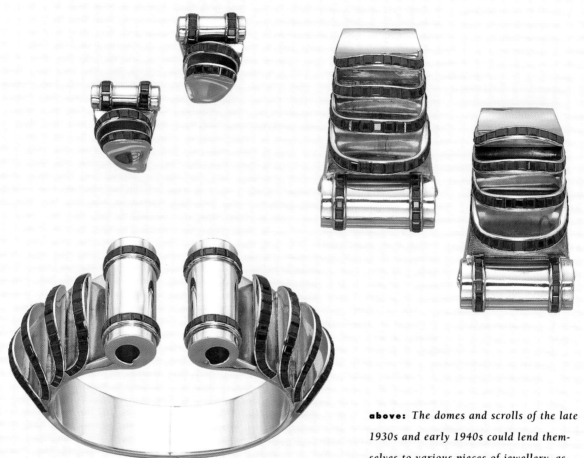

above: *The domes and scrolls of the late 1930s and early 1940s could lend them- selves to various pieces of jewellery, as seen in this gold and ruby suite.*

CULTURED PEARLS

Although Kokichi Mikimoto of Japan is considered to be the king of cultured pearls, the art of creating pearl-covered objects dates back to thirteenth-century China.

At that time small metal or mother-of-pearl carvings were glued in rows to the inside of the shells of river molluscs that, on being returned to the river, coated them with a layer of nacre. The coated carvings were then cut out, complete with the shell backing, and sold as religious souvenirs. In 1896, Kokichi Mikimoto developed the earlier experiments of the eighteenth-century Swedish botanist Carolus Linneaus, and cultivated half-pearls by cementing a half-bead of mother-of-pearl to the inner shell wall of the pearl oyster. It was these half-pearls, also known as "blister" or "mabé" pearls, that were exhibited in Paris in 1900, both on the oyster shell and cut, trimmed and backed for mounting. By 1905, Tokichi Nishikawa of the Japanese Bureau of Fisheries had solved the problem of how to produce round cultured pearls under laboratory conditions, and sold the rights of production to Mikimoto, who was granted a patent for the system in 1916. Mikimoto went on to produce cultured pearls in quantity and to create a successful market for them, helping to meet the demand created in the 1920s by fashion designer Coco Chanel, who reintroduced the pearl as an important fashion accessory for day and evening wear.

Today a cultured pearl is produced by carefully opening the oyster and placing a full mother-of-pearl bead in the soft fleshy part known as the mantle, together with a small piece of mantle tissue from another oyster. As the host oyster rejects the foreign tissue it begins to encyst the bead, coating it with conchiolin and pearl nacre. The best pearls are produced under stringent conditions, and the top cultured-pearl farm are extremely hygienic in order to avoid the pollution problems that occasionally affect Japanese lakes. The molluscs (either oysters or mussels can be used) are carefully tended, and hung in long bunches or cages in calm water of an even temperature – any variation in temperature

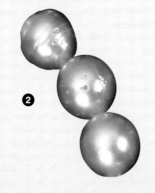

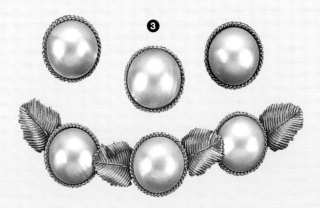

can affect the growth and appearance of the pearl. Some oysters can accommodate several implants at once and are used several times. A growth period of approximately two to three years is needed to produce a good thickness of nacre. Unfortunately, many farms have tried to cut the time down to six months, which results in poor cultured pearls with badly formed, thin skins. In these, the "flash" of the mother-of-pearl bead will be visible through the thin layer of nacre; they will crack more easily; the skin will break away from the bead after drilling; and if badly treated (covered with perfume or hairspray and not cleaned before they are put away) they will deteriorate quickly, leaving a "naked" mother-of-pearl bead. Pearls with thicker skins may be "improved" if required, as blemishes and bumps can be removed by peeling a layer of nacre away, rather like peeling an onion, ideally to reveal a layer underneath that grew under better conditions. Some pearls are bleached, treated and dyed to produce improved colour or fantastical hues of brightness that could not possibly be mistaken for natural.

Distinguishing an imitation pearl from a natural or cultured one is relatively easy. Most are obvious on examination with a jeweller's 10x lens. The imitation usually has a smooth yet slightly granular-looking surface, and can be further identified by the somewhat unhygienic method of rubbing it against one's tooth – it will give a very glassy, smooth response. Older types of imitations look very dull and lifeless and are generally easy to spot. The skins of natural and cultured pearls are identical and differ from the

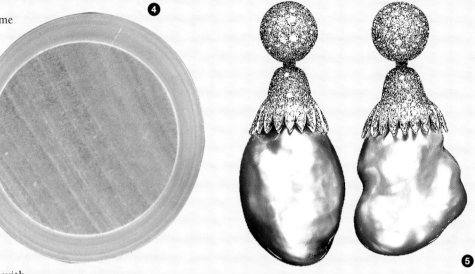

skin of an imitation in that they are made of tiny overlapping platelets of aragonite, the substance that forms nacre. They therefore look uneven under magnification and feel gritty when tooth-tested.

Distinguishing a natural from a cultured pearl is far more problematic. If the cultured pearl is of poor quality the

1 A modern version with pink diamonds, by Christopher Walling, of the thirteenth-century cultured pearls.
2 The skins of these cultured pearls are very poor, but have probably not been left in the oyster long enough to enable them to be peeled.
3 A group of modern mabé cultured pearl jewellery.
4 A section through a cultured pearl, revealing the mother-of-pearl bead centre within the nacre coating.
5 A pair of large cultured pearl and diamond drop earrings by Verdura, an important addition to evening wear.

mother-of-pearl bead nucleus will be obvious. However, it can prove very difficult to tell a good cultured pearl with a thick skin from a natural one. If there is a drill hole it is sometimes possible to see the change in material from nacre to mother-of-pearl, but this can be confused with the changing growth layers seen in a natural pearl, or even just a ring of dirt. The best means of identification is to have the pearls x-rayed at a specialist laboratory where the results can be properly interpreted. However, cultivation methods have progressed and the traditional mother-of-pearl bead nucleus

6 A line of pink conch pearls of varying hues.

7 Part of a cultured pearl necklace composed of baroque shapes; although not the most valuable, many prefer their random shapes.

8 An x-ray of a cultured pearl necklace, clearly showing the mother-of-pearl bead within the pearl.

9 A harlequin necklace.

10 A pair of earrings with ruby and emerald petals around an abalone pearl centre.

11 An x-ray of a natural pearl, seen as a continuous growth, almost tree-like in structure. It is very different to the cultured pearl.

is now being replaced by a small section of mantle tissue alone. The end result can be a very fine cultured pearl with no obvious nucleus detectable by x-ray, which makes origin difficult to determine. These pearls are available at very reasonable prices for necklaces with beads of up to nine millimetres (0.35 inches), but larger pearls rapidly rise in value.

Large, white, nucleated (bead-centred) cultured pearls from a wide area around Australia, Indonesia and the Philippines are marketed as "South Sea" cultured pearls, and generally range in size from nine millimetres to seventeen millimetres (0.35–0.67 inches). The bronze to black varieties from French Polynesia are best known as "Tahitian"

cultured pearls. The growth period for both types is similar to that of their smaller cousins but, unlike the method used in the Japanese and Chinese production of smaller pearls, only one nucleus can be inserted into each mother oyster. Given that some oysters will reject the insert altogether, and that most of the others will produce an off-round or mis-coloured pearl, the production of a large spherical, pure-coloured pearl is still an event of significance and value. Consequently, a strand of well-matched South Sea cultured pearls is a valuable and scarce item.

Increasingly, unusual pearls are appearing on the international market, including abalone pearls in an attractive range of colours; pink-hued conch pearls; and American freshwater pearls, which form strange shapes. Many believe that the best cultured pearls are those with the whitest

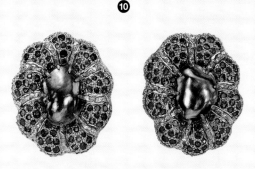

colour; others prefer ones with a rose tint, while the creams can also be popular. It is a matter of personal taste, and as skin colour often dictates which pearl looks best some colours and hues may be more popular on particular continents than on others. The best necklaces are made of pearls that are evenly matched in size and colour, and have blemish-free skins with good lustre (a fine colourful shine rather than a dull surface). Some people, of course, prefer a necklace of various hues or strange baroque shapes, and to that end the so-called less valuable pearls have been cleverly marketed so buyers feel happier about purchasing something previously considered sub-standard. Multicoloured pearls have been strung together to provide "harlequin" necklaces, for example, and ones with a ridged barrel-type appearance, once rejected, are now marketed as "circles of love".

Pearls and cultured pearls have endured numerous changes of fashion over the past century but the different ways in which they can be worn has enabled them to remain constantly admired. This adaptability was superbly de-monstrated by the late Diana, Princess of Wales, when she wore pearls in her hair rather than around her neck, and gave the entire pearl industry a fresh focus.

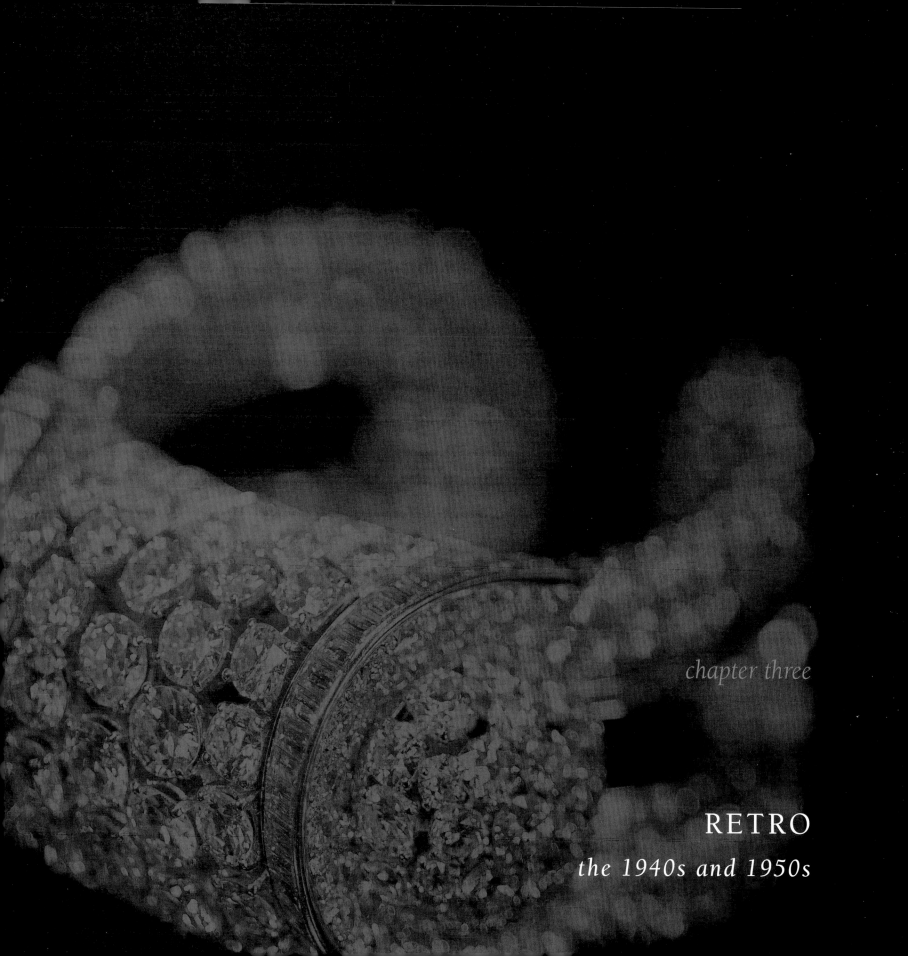

chapter three

RETRO
the 1940s and 1950s

The world war of 1939 to 1945 had a catastrophic effect upon the economies of the combatants and upon their luxury trades in particular, although countries such as the United States, which avoided the appalling damage of direct conflict, still enjoyed an active social scene. War conditions ensured that many diamonds originally intended for the gem market were instead used as the cutting edges of industrial machines to fashion munitions; and the mining and transportation of other gems ceased. Governments took various steps to protect their economies: the Bank of France banned trading in gold in 1940, while in 1942 the Italian Fascist regime banned the sale of precious objects. Refugees were well aware of the importance of concealable high-value commodities, and many gold coins and diamonds were sewn into hems in preparation for the inevitable flight from defeat or persecution. This attitude prevailed throughout the second half of the century whenever there was con-

flict or aggression and jewellery continued to be considered an investment against hard times. Many second-hand and antique pieces were broken up for the value of their gems and precious metals. Fortunately, many fine examples of Art Nouveau and Arts and Crafts jewellery survived, not because they were considered wonderful examples of the jeweller's art but because materials such as enamel, moonstones and citrine had no recoverable value. The edict of style over intrinsic value that provided the basic guidelines for these pieces, produced in relatively small numbers, unwittingly ensured their survival.

above: This brooch by Trabert & Hoeffer-Mauboussin, from 1945, is designed as a V for victory, with the ruby, moonstone and sapphire band, plus the star-set diamonds, representing the American flag.

THE 1940S

Wartime of course generated its own jewellery. As in World War One, regimental badge brooches were produced in quantity, fly-stamped in Birmingham until the factories were destroyed by bombing; or, for the more affluent, crafted in gold and gems by companies such as Garrard of London. Fund-raising efforts were recognized by Spitfire lapel pins and "Bundles for Britain" brooches, and worn proudly to show a contribution had been made to a specific war effort. The Spitfire appeal raised money in Britain to manufacture the badly needed fighter planes, while the Bundles for Britain campaign in the United States encouraged donations of clothes and other much needed commodities for the British civilian population. "Trench art" jewellery was primarily made by soldiers in relatively safe reserve positions behind the front lines, who used shell casings, aircraft canopy Perspex and aluminium, and the popular sentimental jewels also emphasized the patriotism of the wearer. The French jewellers Cartier created the "Bird in a Cage" brooch in 1942 as a symbol of the occupation of France, followed by the "Bird at the Door of the Cage" brooch upon liberation. Another French company, Van Cleef & Arpels, designed a swallow brooch to symbolize the return of spring and freedom, and during German occupation many French jewellers incorporated France's symbol, the proud cockerel, in jewels to signify defiance. After years of jewellery being worn as secret signs and patriotic symbols, brooches modelled as the victory "V", using gems in the national colours, were triumphantly manufactured to celebrate the cessation of the war.

above: *A mid 1940s necklace employing the gas pipe style with ruby-set ball terminals.*

left: *This reverse painted crystal* intaglio *pendant depicts two caged birds, similar to the pieces created by Cartier as a symbol of the occupation of France.*

Women's wartime involvement in factories and industrialization was reflected in the jewellery designs of the mid-1940s including, for example, the "gas pipe" design, inspired by the flexible connections used in military and civilian gas masks, and the many references to machinery in motion. These included features resembling screw heads, ball bearings, tyre tracks and girders. Whereas many bracelets had previously been based on a simple brickwork pattern, a new military influence was now to be seen in the heavier "tank track" designs.

below: This 1940s bangle by Mauboussin illustrates how a large low-value stone with pleats of gold creates an effect of volume without great expenditure.

By the time of the liberation of Paris from German occupation in 1944, the jewellery trade throughout Europe was demoralized and stagnant, supplies were low and many design archives had been destroyed. Low gold stocks necessitated the use of thin stamped sheets in jewellery, and these had to be worked to give maximum effect and incorporate whatever stones were available. These included many of the new man-made synthetics and oversized cheaper gems such as topaz, citrine and aquamarine. The need to make the most of the available gold encouraged much experimentation with varied surface treatments and alloys, one of the more popular being to increase the percentage of copper used to create a pink or rose gold, so that two or more colour golds could be used in the same piece.

The dispersal of craftsmen and designers because of the war meant that jewellery houses struggling to revive their production relied on the styles that had been popular in the late 1930s, adapting these to the availability of materials. Thus the areas previously pavé-set with diamonds or invisibly set with swathes of rubies or sapphires now accommodated aquamarines, amethyst, citrine and topaz, often in fancy cuts. A greater interest and revival in flexible mountings and sprays of *en tremblant* flower heads provided movement in large and colourful floral

sprays. The plumped-out, curved gold leant itself to fabric motifs based on lace and basket-weave in bows, knots, flexible tassels and pleats, and these were set with the pale blue of aquamarine together with the browns and yellows of different shades of citrine, all highlighted by synthetic rubies used not for economy but because of the unavailability of the natural stones. These jewels, of necessity incorporating pre-war designs but with new combinations of colourful gems suitable for wear at less formal events, came to be called "cocktail" or "retro" jewellery, reflecting the love of Hollywood glamour and mood of escapism that swept through gloomy post-war Europe.

With Europe in such a sorry state, luxury goods heavily taxed and populations depressed by the aftermath of war, it is not surprising that attention should have turned to the United States and, in particular, to Hollywood and the movies. The great French jewellery houses saw an opportunity to promote themselves and sought ways of breaking into this market. Mauboussin, for example, formed an alliance with Trabert & Hoeffer Inc. of New York to become jewellers to the stars, including Greta Garbo, Joan Bennett and Hedy Lamar. Cartier, already known as the supplier of exotic jewels to Wallis Simpson, the Duchess of Windsor (see page 77), created a range of cartoon animal and figural jewels. Walt Disney's characters were firmly a part of American culture by the second half of the 1940s, following the success of *Fantasia*, which opened in New York in 1940, and enamelled and jewelled charm bracelets featuring Mickey and Minnie Mouse or Snow White and the Seven Dwarfs became popular fun jewellery. Cartoon animals rubbed lapels with clowns, scarecrows and the ballerina brooch perfected by Van Cleef & Arpels. Rubel Frères, the Parisian manufacturing firm associated with this house,

moved to New York in 1939 shortly after it established a salon in the city. In 1943 their affiliation was dissolved, and Rubel opened independently under his Americanized name John Rubel Co. His company was noted for its baguette (slim rectangular-cut) diamond necklaces and fantasy jewels, including ballerina brooches inspired by the Spanish flamenco dancers who performed at a café in Greenwich Village in New York. Both Van Cleef & Arpels and John Rubel Co. employed Maurice Duvalet as a designer, and it was he who designed the final versions of the ballerina offered by both jewellers after 1943.

The shortage of readily available precious materials, combined with the enjoyment of bold colourful jewels, gave free rein to the mostly American makers of costume jewellery who worked in silver, gilt and paste imitation

above: *One of the original ballerina brooches by John Rubel, c. 1943, set with rubies, sapphires and rose-cut diamonds.*

right: *A 1940s three-colour gold figural brooch of a working cowboy, with ruby-decorated shirt and sapphire-edged chaps.*

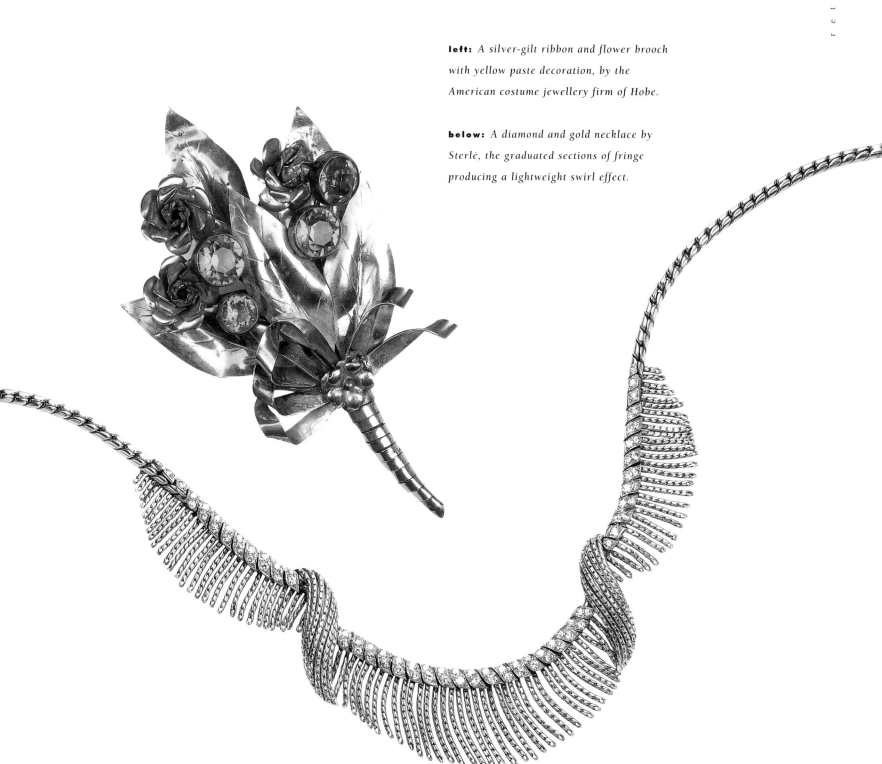

left: *A silver-gilt ribbon and flower brooch with yellow paste decoration, by the American costume jewellery firm of Hobe.*

below: *A diamond and gold necklace by Sterlé, the graduated sections of fringe producing a lightweight swirl effect.*

stones. The reduced cost of these pieces allowed design-ers to create fashion pieces that were affordable to large numbers of women, and which could be worn only a few times and then discarded (see page 144).

Over the second half of the 1940s women's fashion changed again. The more curvaceous 1930s versions of the straight lines encapsulated in 1920s clothes had gone through another transformation in the early 1940s, which resulted in a smart, tailored look that was almost triangu-lar in shape, with strong broad shoulders and a narrow skirt. In the second half of the decade this gave way to the very feminine full skirts and tight tops designed by the newer names in fashion design, including Givenchy and Balenciaga. Christian Dior's influential New Look of 1947 reintroduced colour and volume, and this was reflected in the jewellery of the era, based as it was on floral, textile and nature motifs such as the volute, the three-dimen-sional spiral of the seashell. Designers produced their own particular interpretations. In France Pierre Sterlé created movement and lightness with his woven gold coats of mail, while fellow Frenchman Raymond Templier devel-oped modernist lines with large areas of polished gold and silver. Jean Schlumberger joined Tiffany and Co. of New York as a designer and overturned their traditional atti-tudes by introducing a freedom of design that he had developed while working with clothes designer Elsa Schiaparelli (see page 51). Responding to the shortage of precious metals, Line Vautrin displayed in her shop at 63 Faubourg Saint-Honoré in Paris her remarkable designs for jewellery and accessories in gilt bronze, resin and glass, leading *Vogue* to hail her as a "poetess in metal".

Jeanne Toussaint who had had control of Cartier's *haute joaillerie* since 1933, creating individual designer jewels for exhibition or on commission from clients, was the driving influence behind Cartier's range of jewellery featuring animals and flowers in this period. She was known as "The Panther" (see page 57) and had promoted the black cat as a decorative motif through various exhibitions. In 1948 the Duke of Windsor, in exile in France after his abdication as Edward VIII of Britain in 1936, placed an order with Cartier for a cabochon emer-ald, gold and enamel panther brooch for his wife. This so pleased the duchess that they commissioned several further panthers over the next four years. This created a demand for panther and tiger jewellery among other leading society figures including the Hon. Mrs Fellowes, Princess Nina Aga Khan and Barbara Hutton.

Another fabulous jewel belonging to the Duchess of Windsor was a cuff by Suzanne Belperron, composed of cultured pearls of varied sizes, which was made in the mid-1940s. Pearls had become a great fashion icon from the 1920s onwards, largely due to Coco Chanel who wore them at any time to any function.

left: A citrine and diamond necklace illustrating the favoured colour of the late 1940s and early 1950s.

Japan had enjoyed a growing reputation for the production of cultured pearls prior to World War Two, and this had greatly challenged the natural pearl market and lowered the cost of owning a pearl necklace. By 1939, three hundred and fifty Japanese cultured-pearl farms were producing some ten million pearls annually. A typi-cal necklace of the time was made of pearls generally not exceeding five millimetres (about 0.2 inches) in diameter, and was normally strung as a graduated forty-three centimetre (seventeen inch) necklace with an important seven millimetre (about 0.3 inch) pearl at its centre, down to the three millimetre (about 0.1 inch) pearls at its ends. However, during the war the Japanese government took control of cultured-pearl manufacture, and by 1945 there

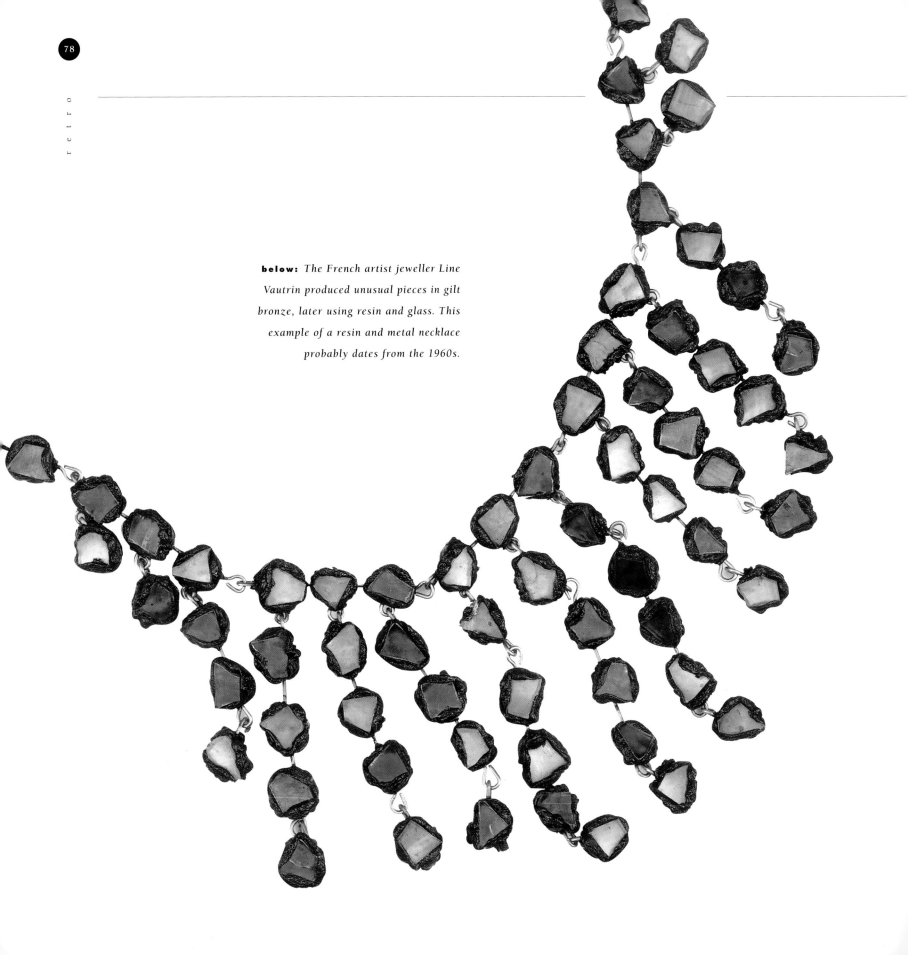

below: *The French artist jeweller Line Vautrin produced unusual pieces in gilt bronze, later using resin and glass. This example of a resin and metal necklace probably dates from the 1960s.*

above: *The cultured pearl and gold cuff by Suzanne Belperron that was made for the Duchess of Windsor.*

left: *This fabulous bird of paradise diamond brooch by Faraone typifies the retro style around the end of the 1940s and could be worn at cocktails or dinner.*

were only one hundred and five farms in operation, all in poor condition. With the Allied occupation of Japan, all transactions were regulated by the Army Exchange Service, and pearls were mainly exported to the United States, which resulted in a postwar revival of the cultured pearl's popularity. By 1948 the industry was free to trade on the open market, and in 1952 production hit ten tonnes for the first time. Other industries were also reviving. In 1947 De Beers purchased the Tanganyika diamond mine from the prospector and explorer Dr John Thorburn Williamson and opened a new plentiful era for the supply of diamonds, matched by gold and gems from South Africa and South America.

The post-war years saw the intermingling of social classes, the emancipation of women and a redistribution of wealth, and gave rise to a new social structure. The art of entertaining also changed as the newly introduced early evening cocktail hour allowed for a greater mixing of the aristocracy, new wealth and celebrities before balls, soirées and formal dinners. Thus the jewellery wardrobe needed to cater for three styles of dress: professional day wear, cocktail wear and formal wear. By the 1950s dress styles for both day and evening were dominated by Christian Dior's opulent New Look, which exchanged the military look of the early 1940s for femininity, with narrow shoulders, cinched waists and emphasized busts and hips. The style reflected the mood of the time, the relief felt at the final conclusion of the war and a new determination to enjoy living. With skirts and dresses reaching mid-calf and requiring luxurious quantities of material, the fashion enraged politicians still set on post-war economies and the

fashion stores that were still holding vast stocks of suddenly outmoded tapered skirts.

Daytime jewellery for the 1950s tended to look back to immediate pre-war influences, and such classics as the Van Cleef & Arpels honeycomb bracelet and invisibly set flower brooches were reintroduced. Gold earrings of clustered leaves or wires set with coloured gems, or dangly creole hoops, accompanied a variety of hairstyles.

Pearls were worn in multiple rows or as long strings

above: *This brooch by Kutchinsky echoes the braid effect by the use of rope design loops with reeded petals and ruby and diamond centres. It is hallmarked London 1959.*

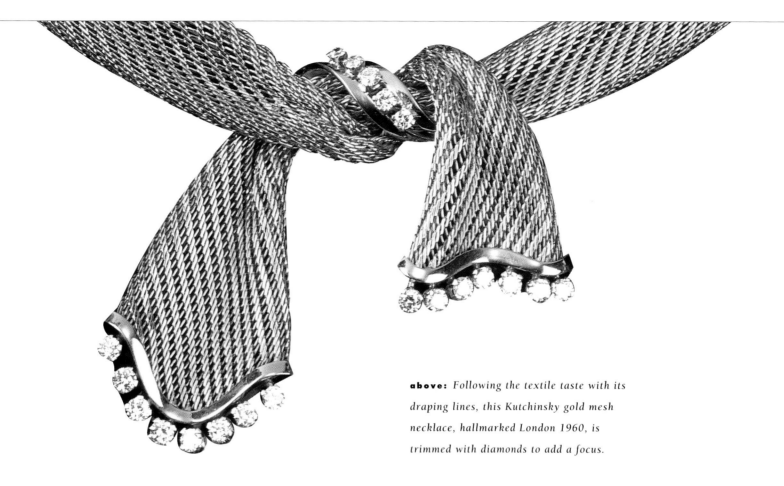

above: *Following the textile taste with its draping lines, this Kutchinsky gold mesh necklace, hallmarked London 1960, is trimmed with diamonds to add a focus.*

wrapped around the neck while daytime brooches, bracelet-watches and rings were practical designs in gold wirework enhanced with minor gems.

Cocktail jewellery was bold, with broad polished gold surfaces worked into curls and loops on large flower sprays. Sometimes the gold was braided, woven into mesh or pierced to imitate ropes, fringes, lace and gauze. Boucheron again caught the spirit of the time with a floral style that featured petals enamelled in the guilloche technique of Fabergé, the gold first engraved or engine-turned and then covered with several thin, translucent layers of enamel. Necklaces were dramatic and included bib styles with their broad fronts set with unexpected combinations of large gems such as amethyst and turquoise to emphasize the décolletage.

Paris was alive with charity balls including the Night of Gems in 1949, followed by the ball given by the fashion designer Jacques Fath and another by Elsa Maxwell, the American celebrity hostess and columnist, at Laurent. At all these prestigious events the women were covered in jewelled birds, flowers and large bows decorated with transparent, stained-glass-like *plique-à-jour* enamel. Gold feathers with scattered coloured gems were fashioned as necklaces and clips, and were usually a little tousled to add realism. A range of "florets" jewellery incorporated flower heads of cabochon sapphires, rubies and

emeralds set in gold braid and platinum. Perhaps the most distinctive 1950s design was the woven gold scarf created by the French writer Jean Cocteau and produced by Boucheron, the fine gold mesh treated as a ribbon of material in folds and drapes with jewelled highlights.

left: *A 1920s chimaera bangle by Van Cleef & Arpels, of carved coral and enamel.*

right: *The later 1950s version of the chimaera bangle shows the carved coral heads to be less fierce than those of its predecessor.*

For formal occasions, diamonds reigned supreme, set as cascading drop necklaces and earrings mounted in articulated and stepped platinum settings to provide depth and movement. Bracelets, brooches and bracelet-watches were also encrusted with diamonds in a variety of drop-shaped, rectangular baguette and spear-point cuts supporting the circular brilliant cuts, which were often set in graduated lines. Tiaras also returned to fashion, but now tended to be inverted necklaces worn on a detachable frame rather than a single-use hair ornament.

At Cartier, Jeanne Toussaint reintroduced the Chimaera bangle for 1954. The fabulous oriental monster, double-headed bangles had first been produced in the Art Deco period. At that time, the love of jewellery inspired by India had turned attention to the traditional makara, a double-headed bangle based on the Indian crocodile. Cartier replaced the crocodile heads with the oriental "kilin", a mythical winged monster, although in some cases he did retain the typical floral enamel decoration to the body. Carved coral examples with fearsome heads were produced from 1922 to 1929, but for the 1950s the expressions were modified to those of a friendly and beguiling pet, and were carved in salmon-pink coral or lapis lazuli or set throughout with precious gems. These bracelets were evidence of the resources available to Cartier for the realization of exciting designs. The house's requirements were fulfilled by specialist dealers who supplied high-quality materials at high prices. The lapis

left: *A diamond and multi-gem suite of jewellery from the late 1940s, photographed against the original design drawings.*

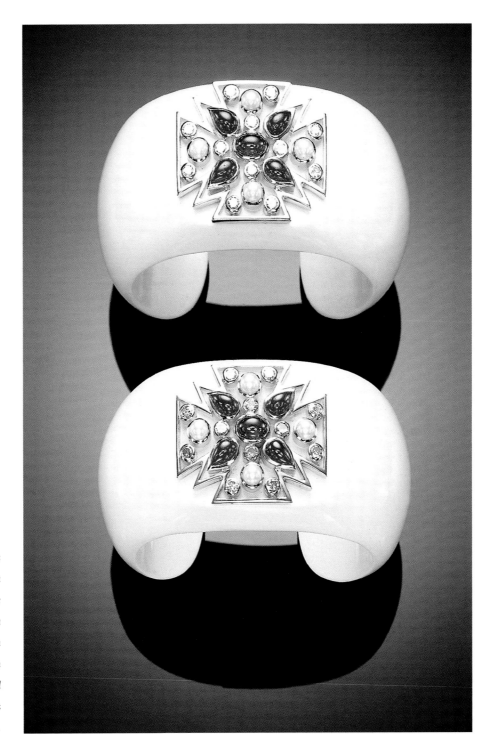

right: *A pair of bangles designed by Verdura for Chanel, baked white enamel that Verdura called cocholong, each Maltese cross set with diamonds, cultured pearls, rubies and sapphires.*

lazuli was purchased from the Russian dealer Isaharoff, and the Japanese coral was imported through Italy to the specialist agent Bonelli of Paris. The coral had to be supplied in large stalks so that the hooped bracelets could be produced in two curved pieces, despite the fact that the usual practice was to set many smaller sections together as this avoided the waste of good material caused by a single carving. The carving was entrusted to the workshop of Louis Bozzachi who had previously worked for Fabergé. A single bangle required approximately two hundred and fifty to three hundred hours of skilled craftsmanship, and was then sent to Cartier's Lavabre workshop for completion. Such quality and ostentation was appreciated by society leaders in both the United States and Europe, including the Hon. Mrs Fellowes, daughter of the third Duc Descazes, and Isabelle Blanche Singer, heiress of the Singer Sewing Machine millions.

Other creatures also emerged from Cartier, including a dolphin bangle in white and yellow gold introduced in 1959 and the ever-popular panther. Princess Nina Aga Khan became a keen collector of panther jewellery, beginning in 1957 with an outstretched panther jabot pin, for the ruffle at the front of a dress, clasped by a thirty-carat sapphire similar in style to the Duchess of Windsor's present from the duke in 1948 (see page 77). Over the next three years she acquired a complete parure of flexible panther pendant, panther-head bangle and ear clips, a coiled panther ring and, to complete the ensemble, an evening bag with a gold panther handle, which also doubled as another bangle. For the American Barbara Hutton, the world's richest heiress, Jeanne Toussaint created a tiger with stripes in yellow diamonds and onyx, the stones set so closely together that little of the metal was visible – the style known as "pavé set".

The vast buying power of the American elite was well served by branches of the French houses in New York, including Cartier, Van Cleef & Arpels, Mauboussin and Chaumet, together with the American companies of Tiffany (with designer Jean Schlumberger), Harry Winston, Verdura, Webb, and Black, Starr and Frost. Harry Winston, the king of diamonds who provided important stones for stars of screen and society, perhaps best served the desire for glamour so prevalent in 1950s America. Since founding his company in 1932 he had, through his skill, knowledge and love of fine diamonds, created his own style, crafting an array of gems into superb jewellery mounted in fine, flexible platinum-wire settings. He was responsible for the cutting of such famous diamonds as the Jonker, the Taylor-Burton, the Star of Sierra Leone and the Vargas. He also donated the Hope, the Portuguese and the Oppenheimer diamonds to the Smithsonian Institution in Washington.

left: *An unusual example of the popular panther jewellery, modelled as a skin rug; the amethyst is surrounded by black enamel spots, with pearl eyes and diamond collar.*

right: *This c.1950 Cartier ring incorporates a line of coral miniature cocktail shakers, each with a diamond top – a real cocktail ring.*

The Sicilian Duke Fulco di Verdura had arrived in Paris from his native Palermo in 1926 to work as a textile designer for Coco Chanel. She soon recognized his talent and appointed him her head jewellery designer. He redesigned her collection of outdated jewellery, and his dramatic cuff bangles and gold-braid earrings established a theme that was to flower over the coming years. In 1934, Verdura moved to the United States with his friend Baron Nicolas de Gunzberg to establish a jewellery design workshop and the aristocratic backgrounds of both men led to introductions to important members of society in New York, Hollywood and Palm Beach. The New York jeweller Paul Flato used Verdura's designs with such success that when he decided to expand to Los Angeles in 1937 he chose Verdura to run his new gallery there. Here the duke was in his theatrical element, befriending many film stars including James Stewart, Gary Cooper, Marlene Dietrich and Rita Hayworth. With this army of enthusiasts, and the financial support of songwriter Cole Porter, he opened his own business on Fifth Avenue back in New York in 1939. He was fortunate that the war did not impinge on the American social scene and his business prospered, his circle of admirers and clients extending to the Duchess of Windsor, Marjorie Merriweather

below: Verdura turned this scallop shell into a brooch with the addition of diamond-set platinum tendrils.

Post and British actor Laurence Olivier. He also collaborated with surrealist artist Salvador Dalí in a collection of painted jewels. Commissions flowed in for pieces for special occasions and presentations, including, in the 1950s, one for a tiara for Betsy Hay Witney to wear when presented at court on the appointment of her husband John as the ambassador to the Court of St James's in London. On this occasion Verdura's design, with its golden feathers rising from a diamond circlet, was based on an American Indian headdress. In 1952 he began an association with André Chervin, a highly skilled enameller who had the ability to create designs exactly as envisaged by Verdura, and his artistic influence became recognized by designers as diverse as Jean Schlumberger, Kenneth Jay Lane, David Webb and Paloma Picasso. His work was full of innovation and humour, and incorporated fruit, flowers and animals created in exquisite detail. He delighted in pearls and brightly coloured gems, but kept diamonds to a minimum. In the 1940s he had started to create jewels centred on a seashell or pebble and in the 1950s these, together with his signature braided rope, launched a craze for shell jewels across the United States. Jean Schlumberger had joined Tiffany in New York as a designer after World War Two, and was appointed vice-president in 1956. Like Verdura, he was inspired by *objets trouvés* such as pebbles, shells and seed pods, and by bright

above: *A pair of enamelled gold bracelets incorporating the well-known kiss design, an example of the slightly later work of Jean Schlumberger c. 1960.*

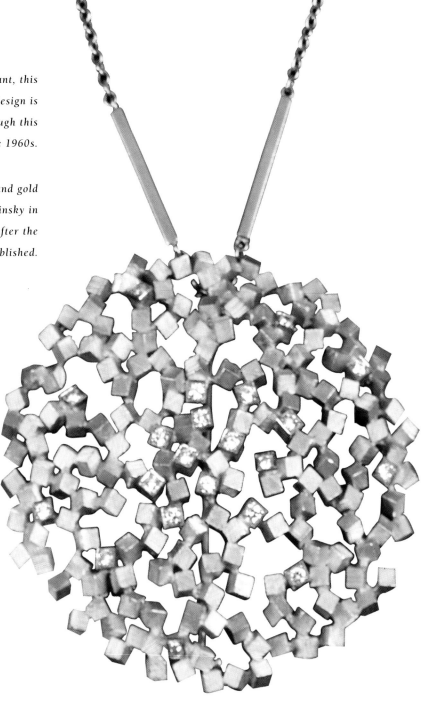

right: *A John Donald pendant, this small block and diamond design is typical of his work, although this example dates from the 1960s.*

far right: *This diamond and gold brooch was made by Joe Kutchinsky in the late 1950s shortly after the London shop was established.*

colours, to create exotic jewels that diverged enormously from the traditional Tiffany range, and his admirers eagerly awaited each new design. He was the first of Tiffany's designers to be permitted to apply his own signature to his creations, and his work is much sought after today. The Danish firm of Georg Jensen brought sculptural jewellery to the United States by establishing and exhibiting the Lunning prize for Scandinavian design in 1951. During the 1950s, winners included the fluid abstract designs of Henning Koppel and Nana Ditzel presaging the mixture of art and sculpture in jewellery that was to be a hallmark of 1960s design. Individual designers were given encouragement by the institution of the De Beers Diamond International Awards in 1954, which promoted innovative design and saw the rise of such names as John Donald, David Thomas, Geoffrey Turk and Podalsky. In Italy, the Pomodoro brothers,

Arnaldo and Giorgio, created both sculpture and sculptural jewels; and in Spain and in France painters Salvador Dalí and Georges Braque both designed unique jewellery.

Van Cleef & Arpels embarked upon a new era of marketing when, in 1954, they introduced their "boutique" department. This specialized in easily worn jewellery for their fashion-conscious clientele, who wished to be at the height of fashion and wear a good

left: *The shape of this abstract design gold bird brooch echoes that made famous by Georges Braque.*

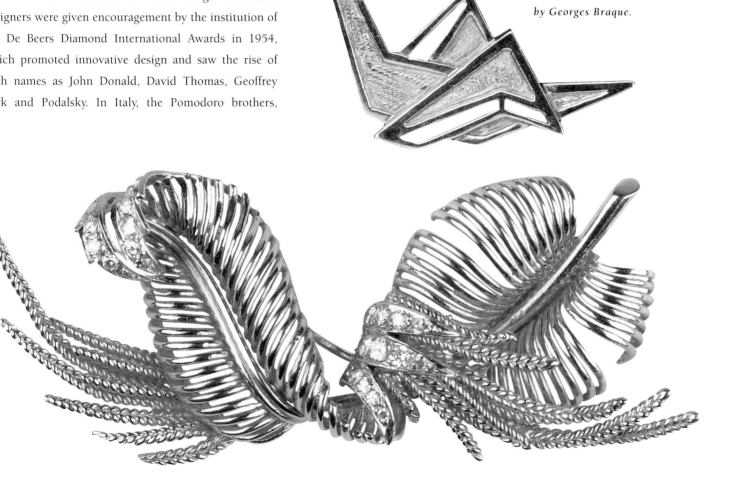

tour of France, the United States, Sweden and Russia in 1958, he had established the knowledge and contacts he needed to move his business from his workshop supplying the trade in the East End of London to his own premises in Knightsbridge, close to the world-famous Harrods store. His reputation grew rapidly, based on personal service, innovative stock and an opulent quality that was ensured by manufacturing in his own Denman Street workshops in London's Soho. He was well placed to serve the needs of the new breed of entrepreneurial businessmen who had made money catering for the massive demand in home furnishing and equipment as post-war redevelopment got under way. His stock ranged from the extravagant diamond and baguette-diamond scroll and cascade evening jewellery to amusing gold, enamel and hardstone animal brooches, including chunky panthers and leopards that were distinctly different from the sophisticated Cartier products.

The coming space age had been symbolized by the flying-saucer-shaped Dome of Discovery pavilion at the Festival of Britain in 1951, but was brought to everybody's notice by the launch on 4 October 1957 of the Soviet Union's Sputnik I, followed on 3 November by Sputnik II carrying the dog Laika. The space race between the United States and Russia had started and the public was fascinated by technological and scientific developments. These were symbolized by the centrepiece of the "Universal Exhibition" in Brussels in 1958 – the Atomium building, modelled on a molecule of iron. This molecular design was used in a presentation ring by the jeweller David Webb of New York, the designer of many gold, enamel and gem fantasy pieces, including spiky Sputnik and rocket designs, all of which were to catch the futuristic mood of the coming decade.

left: *David Webb made this diamond and gold ring, inspired by the Atomium building at the Universal Exhibition in Brussels, in 1958.*

right: *This diamond brooch from the late 1950s is a good example of cascade or waterfall jewellery.*

class of jewel but did not want to spend as much as would be required to buy in the main house. Public awareness of the quality of the gems they were buying was also being promoted with the introduction in 1957 of diamond-grading certificates, a first small step on a rapidly developing road.

The British jewellery trade had been strangled throughout the 1950s by a purchase tax on new jewellery of over one hundred per cent. Consequently the trade had been almost entirely in second-hand goods, but one Joe Kutchinsky was determined to create and market his own style. After a study

above: *The space race influence is seen in this watch by Le Coultre from 1955. It has a feeling of planets revolving at speed.*

SYNTHETIC GEMS AND GEM TREATMENTS

One of the many industrial advances of the late nineteenth century was discovering how to produce intense heat by combining oxygen and hydrogen gases. In 1891, Auguste Verneuil developed a vertical oxy-hydrogen blowtorch encased in a furnace through which he fed aluminium oxide powder and a powdered colouring agent to create synthetic (man-made) sapphires and rubies.

This was the first time that gems had been chemically analysed and then actually replicated, rather than merely imitated, by man. Consequently, the synthetic gems produced in the early part of the twentieth century were hailed as technological marvels and were often mounted in the centre of valuable jewels as a conversation piece. There was also a huge demand in the late 1940s for synthetic rubies and sapphires for jewellery due to the scarcity of natural gems, so most period pieces from this era contain verneuil synthetics. These are relatively easy to identify in nearly all but the very smallest sizes, as under magnification the circular growth lines (rather like the grooves on a record), and sometimes bubbles, can be seen. Synthetic gems are also used as the "jewels" found in watch movements, and for industrial and medical lasers.

The colour of a gemstone may be derived from the elements that make up its basic atomic structure. In some cases this is part of the formation of the gem – for example, the green colour of peridot comes from the iron element in its composition so all peridot will be some shade of green. In other stones the colouring agents, such as vanadium and chromium, which colour sapphires and rubies, are natural additions to the basic structure of the family group corundum, so colours can range from white (colourless, in fact) through yellow, green, blue and red depending on the chemical composition of the stone. The practice of heating gems to disturb their composition and improve the depth and saturation of colour, or change purple amethyst to yellow citrine for example, traces its roots back to the Romans. The ancient Roman practice of heating and then quenching quartz (immersing it in cold water) to produce crazing

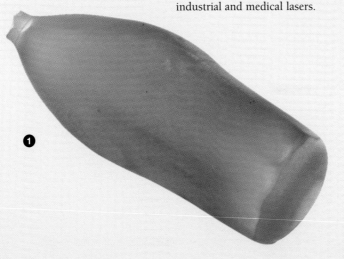

1

2

1 A man-made boule of synthetic sapphire, still produced in laboratories today.

2 Dating from the late 1940s or early 1950s, this diamond bracelet is set with synthetic rubies, a typical feature of the period.

3 The natural features seen in the more recently developed methods of synthetic crystal growth make identification more difficult.

4 An example of the fine lines seen in verneuil synthetics.

cracks that can be dyed is an established and accepted procedure. More recently, heat treatment has been combined with advances in technology for different purposes. For example, a late twentieth-century discovery was that silky white "Gueda" sapphires from Sri Lanka could be permanently turned a good commercial blue with the relatively easy application of the correct heat treatment, suddenly creating a market for what was previously mine waste.

The problem for the consumer is how the value and origin of a stone is established, and how to tell whether it has been treated or is naturally formed. A treated stone cannot be worth as much as a remarkable product of nature. Is the stone therefore worth only the cost of the poor-quality rough material, plus treatment, plus profit, or is it worth a percentage of its similar natural cousin? Because successful heat treatment can only be detected by detailed internal examination of the gem in a laboratory, it has now become common practice for all important coloured gemstones to be accompanied by a certificate stating the degree of treatment varying from none (rare), through minimal and moderate, to severe. As the treatment level increases, the value decreases.

Other less acceptable effects can be created during heat treatment if materials are added to the gems. By including additional vanadium in the furnace environment, for example, sapphires can be diffused with a thin film of colour that binds itself to the outer skin of the stone, giving a much-improved appearance but one that is literally only skin deep.

Rubies may be heat-treated in a borax flux to fill their cavities and fissures with borax glass, which melts into the stone and improves its surface. This becomes even more problematic when artificial colouring agents are added to the flux to improve the body colour of the stone. Emeralds, which commonly have surface-reaching fissures, have traditionally been treated with oils such as Canada Balsam to improve transparency, a reversible and

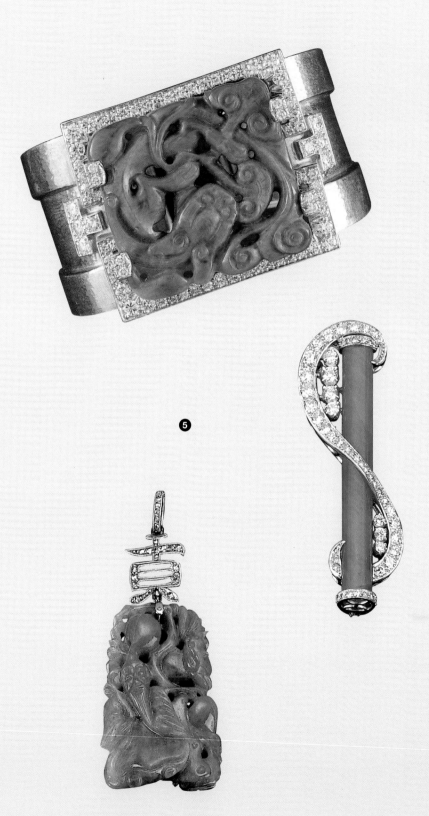

5

renewable treatment. However, recent developments have included the introduction of coloured resins under vacuum, which give a false and unstable "improvement" to the gem. Similarly, fractures in diamonds are being filled with a pressure-induced resin, while black inclusions are lightened by laser treatment, which leaves a fine tubular track to the site of the inclusion that may subsequently be filled.

Diamonds have historically been considered impervious to improvement or reproduction, but the demand for stones for industry during World War Two initiated a series of experiments into the synthesis of diamonds, that is, the artificial production of these stones in the laboratory. The 1950s saw results, first in Sweden and then in the well-documented breakthrough by the General Electric Company of New York in 1955, which led to the mass production of synthetic industrial diamonds for which size and clarity were not an issue. It was not until 1970 that GEC first produced a one-carat, gem-quality synthetic diamond, and it was at a production cost that far exceeded that of the mined natural stone.

5 These natural colour jade pieces range from good (centre) to moderate in colour, but many others have had treatments that are difficult to detect.

6 This diamond has been graded as D colour and internally flawless; weighing over five carats it is an important stone.

7 A certificate accompanies this fourteen-carat sapphire to prove that it has not been subjected to any enhancements, not even the commonly occurring heat treatment.

8 This eighteen-carat emerald has been certified as having evidence of faint clarity enhancement by the use of oils.

These experiments led to a greater understanding of the natural formation of diamonds, so these conditions can now be reproduced in the laboratory, and diamonds in the yellow to brown series (see page 185) are now being subjected to a high-temperature, high-pressure treatment known as HTHP, which can improve their colour grading by decreasing the tint in a way that duplicates the formation of diamonds in nature. This, together with the appearance on the market of gem-quality synthetic diamonds, means that even the hardest and purest of gems must now be considered with caution. The fact that the big four – diamond, ruby, sapphire and emerald – are all subject to a range of treatments, some of which cannot be considered stable, has led to a loss of confidence among consumers, and a move towards such stones as

tourmaline, peridot and new coloured garnets that can correctly be described as untreated. In Asia the same problems are to be found in the jade market, where much so-called B-Jade, as opposed to the top quality A-Jade, has been bleached, dyed or polymer-impregnated so that the apparent colour may, in the worst cases, be entirely artificial.

The great majority of gemstones now offered for sale have been "improved" in some manner and, providing that the treatment is stable, is reflected in the selling price of the gem and is clearly documented, this does allow far more consumers to enjoy wearing jewellery at affordable prices. However, more education of the buying public is required in order for them to understand the many variables involved in defining the quality of a gem.

chapter four

STREET FASHION

the 1960s and 1970s

THE 1960S

The 1960s was the decade of youth revolution, of miniskirts and hot pants, psychedelic colours and jarring contrasts. Many women had previously been fitted by dressmakers, and viewed formal poise and grooming as an important part of their image, but now they bought their wardrobe from the mainstream shops, and dress styles became more casual. Every established idea was turned upside down, and a new culturally influential voice was to be heard, that of the teenager. The emergence of the teenager was accompanied by revolutionary new music by bands such as The Beatles, and by new younger icons including models such as the British Twiggy who rose to fame at the age of sixteen. Make-up styles were no longer haughtily sophisticated, but sought to create a wide-eyed innocence that produced the baby-doll look. Second-hand clothes became acceptable and no longer the province of the poor, and were mixed with experimental new designs that incorporated and explored new materials. Anything could be used, resulting in dresses made of PVC, leather or discs of plastic or metal. In the United States the hippie movement culminated in 1967 with the "Summer of Love", bringing together all those groups who wished to detach themselves from established society. In some cases society followed – designer Jean Bouquin created Hippie Deluxe for the jet set of St Tropez. The demands of young trendsetters with few resources were met by a surge of inexpensive stylish clothes and jewellery mass-produced for outlets such as Carnaby Street in London.

The elegance of the 1950s was shattered and replaced, in the extreme, by a desire to shock. This was mirrored in the jewellery world, and the division between *haute joaillerie* (established jewellers such as Cartier and Boucheron) and the studio jewellers (independent designer/manufacturers) became more pronounced, leading to many aspects of jewellery being questioned. The reliance upon traditional cut gemstones was challenged by the use of natural crystal clusters or single crystals, used as found, gold rubbed shoulders with plastic and new methods of manufacture created different surface effects. With the end of the 1960s came jewels that were no longer merely ornamental, but also functioned as sculptures, clothing or sociopolitical statements.

While *haute joaillerie* continued the tradition of using precious materials such as gold and diamonds, studio jewellers began to produce work that was both innovative in design and yet still pleased the establishment. British studio jewellers were well aware of the conservatism of the buying public and needed to balance boundary-pushing with wearability. This was well

below: *Designs in the 1960s became more space-age, as seen in this platinum and diamond brooch by Heinz Wipperfeld, c. 1965.*

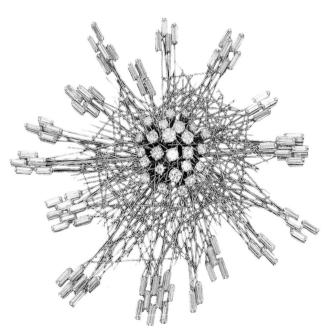

above: *A set of sapphire and emerald "Algae" jewellery by Rene Boivin, from 1962, illustrating the love of organic shapes prevalent in the 1960s.*

understood by Andrew Grima, who based his designs on objects from nature, repeating the theme using rough slate and fish-tank style windows in his salon in Jermyn Street, London. Charles de Temple, son of the famous American cowboy silent film star Tom Mix, used gold to

above & below: *The crossover of modern and traditional is recognised in this sapphire and diamond set by Gunter Wyss, c. 1965.*

"wrap" cultured pearls, creating soft organic forms that looked like pearls held by fronds of seaweed. Gillian Packard, meanwhile, took her inspiration from contemporary artists such as Ben Nicholson and worked in variously coloured golds with subtle textures and layered structures.

The sculptural qualities of gold were well understood by designer/sculptor Bjorn Weckstrom who worked for the influential Lapponia Jewellery Company of Helsinki, Finland. He created textured finishes on gold and silver jewels using a new casting technique of wax injection in rubber moulds, which allowed greater flexibility in the shapes and surface textures that were produced. His jewellery is very distinctive, with its blocky industrial and space age shapes, and had the effect of greatly enhancing the international reputation of Scandinavian design during this period. Another great boost to Scandinavian

design was the "The Arts of Denmark, Viking to Modern" exhibition held in the Metropolitan Museum of Art in New York in 1960. The display included contemporary silverware and jewellery by craftsmen such as Nanna and Jorgen Ditzel, Erik Herlow, Georg Jensen, Henning Koppel, Harald Nielsen and John Rohde. This highly successful exhibition established Danish design in particular as a leading influence in the jewellery world.

Regard for the Danes was further demonstrated when the Worshipful Company of Goldsmiths in London held the Georg Jensen Centenary Exhibition in Goldsmiths Hall in 1966 in order to encourage and inspire modern craftsmen. Jensen, a renowned Danish jeweller, had died in 1935 but, as the exhibition illustrated, the Georg Jensen Company continued to produce innovative designs after his death. It is a company that has employed many artist designers over the years, but perhaps the best known from the 1960s is Henning Koppel.

Koppel replaced the ornamental naturalistic forms for which Jensen was known with biomorphic shapes based on free-flowing amoeba with brightly polished enamel surfaces; and he was in part responsible for establishing "Scandinavian Modern" style. His versatility was recognized at the New York Diamond International

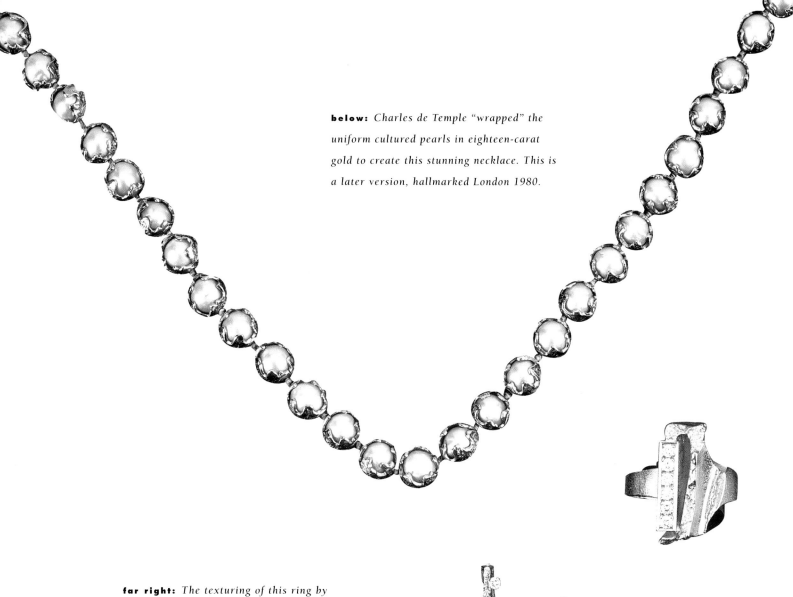

below: *Charles de Temple "wrapped" the uniform cultured pearls in eighteen-carat gold to create this stunning necklace. This is a later version, hallmarked London 1980.*

far right: *The texturing of this ring by the Finnish firm Lapponia gives the impression of molten metal, a style with which they are easily identified.*

right: *An eighteen-carat gold textured abstract design brooch by Gillian Packard from 1970.*

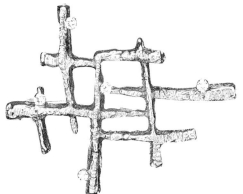

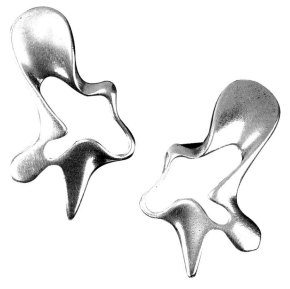

above: A pair of silver earrings by jewellers Georg Jensen, the amoebic form typifying the firm's later work.

Competition in 1966, at which his designs won three out of the twenty-one awards. Jensen's reputation was further enhanced by the work of another designer, Vivianna Torun Bulow-Hube, who joined the company in 1967. Prior to this she had run design studios in Stockholm (Sweden), France, Germany and Indonesia at various periods from 1951 onwards. Working at Jensen in the late 1960s, she produced a range of graceful, clean-lined jewellery that incorporated smooth polished stones typifying the modern Scandinavian jewel.

The First International Exhibition of Modern Jewellery 1860–1961 was held at Goldsmiths' Hall in London in October 1961. It featured many innovations, including the original "princess" cut for diamonds (subsequently renamed the "profile" cut). This produced quite thin slices of diamond, the underside cut with a series of parallel lines, and provided a larger visible expanse of diamond for less material and therefore at a lower cost. Designers at the exhibition included the influential Andrew Grima, John Donald, Louis Osman, Gillian Packard and David Thomas. Many of the pieces on show incorporated natural uncut crystals, minerals and stones of minor value in mounts derived from organic shapes such as branches and fronds. They challenged preconceived ideas that jewellery was a display of status and required of those who saw them the discernment to appreciate them as works of art.

The more traditional jewellers adapted subtly to the new styles, and some looked to the past for their inspiration. The art of goldsmithing was enjoying a post-war renaissance and craftsmen around the world looked both forward to new technology and back towards past cultures. Ancient Greece had been one of the cradles of jewellery production, and it was a museum display of brooches from Mycenae that first inspired the young Greek designer Ilias Lalaounis to reproduce ancient pieces. His first exhibition at the 1957 Thessalonika International Fair aroused criticism because of his slavish copying of old pieces. Realizing that he must put his own interpretation into the ancient designs, he learnt the following crafts: granulation (the fine art of applying tiny beads); repoussé chasing (where the work is raised

below: The original style of naturalistic forms seen in this early Jensen bracelet is still popular.

above: *Typical of the work of Andrew Grima, this pendant with textured eighteen-carat gold surround incorporates a dioptase crystal group.*

right: *This diamond necklace, the first to use the new princess cut, was displayed at the International Exhibition of Jewellery at Goldsmiths' Hall, London, in 1961.*

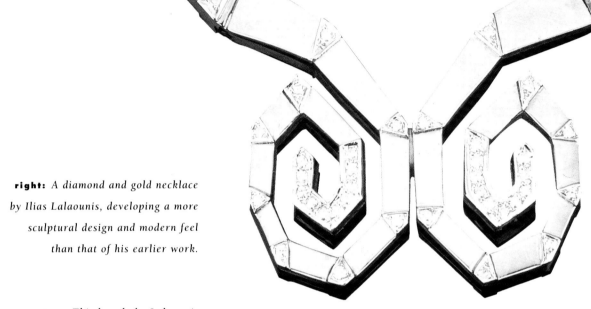

right: *A diamond and gold necklace by Ilias Lalaounis, developing a more sculptural design and modern feel than that of his earlier work.*

below: *This bangle by Lalaounis shows the influence of traditional Greek jewellery.*

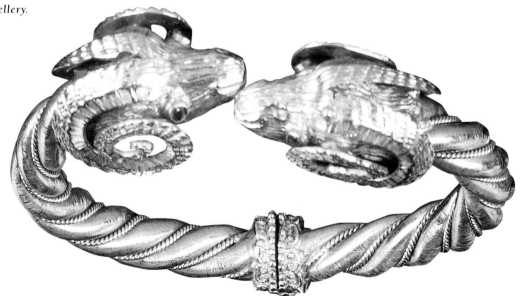

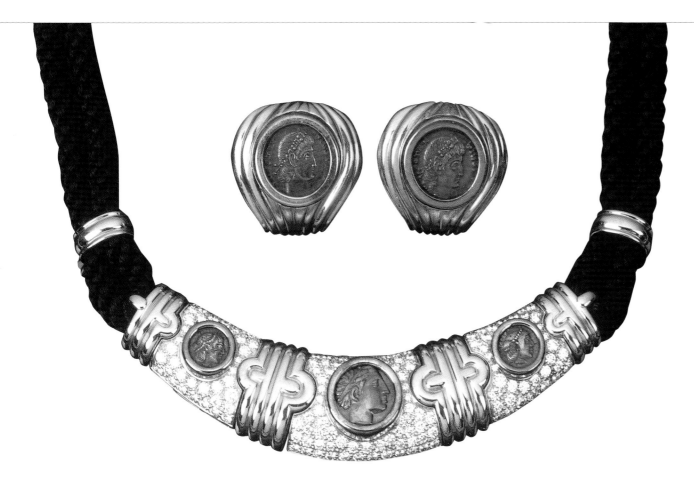

from the back); and the hand-hammering of gold. He also studied examples of sculpture, frescoes, mosaics and icons in detail to grasp the spirit of ancient Greece. As his work became known and popular, particularly following the purchase of wedding gifts from his salon in 1968 by the Greek tycoon Aristotle Onassis for his wife-to-be Jacqueline Bouvier Kennedy, his sources of inspiration widened to embrace other cultures, nature and science. However, his jewellery continued to embody the lessons in style and construction he learnt from studying the work of the ancient Greek goldsmiths.

Bulgari, the influential and well-established fashion house, now under the guidance of Giorgio, the son of its founder Sotiro, also grasped the challenge to break away from conventional styles and produced a range of jewels inspired by classical and Renaissance art, featuring the colours and patterns found in mosaics. Set with brightly coloured cabochon gems in handcrafted gold bezels within a frame of tapered baguette diamonds, the whole encased in a heavy gold chain, they created a vibrant compact style well suited to the ruling fashions of European high society. The unusual colour combinations created by the mixture of stones were reflected in the variety of metals used for the mounts, which included coloured golds in conjunction with polished and burnished steel. Also launched in the 1960s were Bulgari's ancient-coin pieces, set with

above: *A Greek influence is seen in these Bulgari jewels, the gold and diamond mounts being set with ancient Greek coins, this slightly later examples dates from c. 1980.*

Greek and Roman silver coins that were identified on the reverse of the mount. This was by no means a new idea as older elements, including ancient coins, had been incorporated in jewellery made in the nineteenth century. Such coins were, and still are, plentiful and therefore of fairly limited commercial value, but they add an interesting twist to an otherwise very modern look, which inspired cheap copies. Bulgari designers did not only look to the past for inspiration. They also drew ideas from the rapidly expanding industrial activities around them. The sprung flexible gas pipe reappeared in alternating colours, and was used in a full matching range of Bulgari jewellery including the popular bracelet-watches where its numerous coils terminated at the (usually round) watch head.

Throughout the 1960s *haute joaillerie* continued to produce impressive diamond and gem jewellery for their clients – who were also increasingly appreciative of high-quality antique jewellery, especially if it was with good provenance. Both clients and jewel houses were therefore excited when the end of the decade witnessed the first of Christie's sales of jewellery at the Hotel Richemond in Geneva on 1 May 1969. The high levels of customs duty and Value Added Tax levied in Britain made it increasingly difficult to sell imported goods and works of art under one hundred years old in London, forcing Christie's to look at the tax-free selling centres of Switzerland and Hong Kong. Geneva was the site chosen for a sale to offer jewels from some important estates, including an antique diamond corsage from the collection

above: Bulgari promoted jewellery sets with cabochon gems of various colours, typified by this later version of peridot, pink and green tourmaline, amethyst and citrine.

right: A combination of two famous Bulgari styles, the "Bulgari Bulgari" watch on a coiled Tubogas bracelet.

left: *The important black pearl necklace sold in Christie's Geneva in 1969.*

of H.M. Queen Marie-José of Italy. One of the highlights of the sale was a three-row, natural black pearl necklace (see previous page) incorporating pearls from the necklace of Catherine the Great of Russia, which was subsequently owned by Princess Tatiana Youssoupoff and Lady Deterding. The necklace was sold from the estate of Nina Dyer, wife of Baron Heinrich Thyssen and later of Prince Sadruddin Aga Khan, and realized an outstanding $135,000. When it was offered again at Christie's Geneva in 1997 it achieved a staggering $893,000. The sale established a pattern of highly important auctions, which has continued to the present day, by providing a sumptuous collection of top-quality jewels available to a worldwide audience.

below: An example of Art Deco revival produced as a piece of costume jewellery by Kenneth Jay Lane, c. 1972.

THE 1970S

Big and bold was the theme for the major jewellery houses in the 1970s. Despite the rising price of gold, jewellery was chunky, incorporating the strong colours of coral, onyx and lapis, and set with diamonds in yellow gold. Fashion was free from restraint – the French designer Paco Rabanne even developed aluminium chain-mail wedding dresses. In Britain, designer Zandra Rhodes accessorized her 1970s collections with costume jewellery by Mich Milligan, and fashion designer Vivienne Westwood collaborated with Tom Binns who produced punk design jewellery to accompany her clothes. Lifestyles were far freer and more casual, jeans were for everyone and charter flights opened up the world. The 1970s was the decade of anarchy in both fashion and music. Glam rock encouraged men to wear make-up and jewels while punk highlighted body decoration, if only with safety pins. Anarchy also ruled amongst the young designer jewellers, who tore up the rule books and created emphatic jewellery in paper, feathers, plastic and iron using vacuum-forming and industrial presses to realize their bold images. Many of these pieces were ephemeral stage or catwalk productions that did not attempt to compete with the mainstream jewellery stores, which offered bold costume jewellery beside the still-popular gold and gems.

As strong as this new wave was in going forward, there still seemed room for a look back to previous years and the fashions that went with it. In London, a boutique called Biba had opened in the mid-1960s with more than a hint of Art Deco about its design and contents, and this

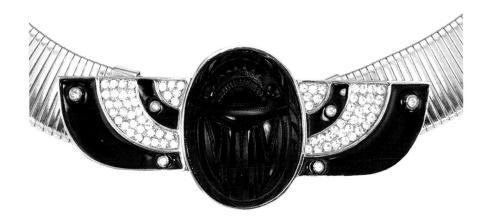

left: *A necklace and earring set by Chaumet, c. 1970, continuing the molten metal theme on large discs and clean lines.*

link with the past was further emphasized when, in 1973, the boutique took over an old department store and retained the original Deco interior. Jewellery followed suit, and Deco-style pieces of costume jewellery were sold in the 1960s and 1970s in Biba and many of the other new outlets that had opened to cater for the fashion-conscious young. There was also a flood of cheap brightly coloured fun jewellery, to accompany the glam-rock look, which was not to be taken seriously. Make-up of the 1970s reflected the Art Deco theme, with its large eyes and bee-stung lips. London led the fashion scene, which was centred around the top shopping locale Carnaby Street and was put on the international youth-style map by The Beatles and Twiggy, the famous British model – her wide-eyed face and skinny figure flattered the designs of the early 1970s to the extent that she appeared with David Bowie on the cover of his 1973 album *Pin Ups*.

above: *Kenneth Jay Lane's costume jewellery necklace uses black and white as negative and positive, and the points give a spike-like feel that fitted the late 1970s' punk era.*

The miniskirt of the 1960s was replaced in the 1970s with the "midi", the new longer-length skirt that reached mid-calf. This more relaxed look continued until the spring of 1977 and the arrival of punk. Punk was a deliberately cheap, scruffy and trashy look, characterized by body piercing, which was no longer restricted to the ears – noses, lips and eyebrows were pierced to sport the trademark safety pin and beads. With spiky, fluorescent coloured hair, disaffected punk youth demonstrated its denial of conformity and belief in an anarchic new world order. In the big name fashion houses this style was slightly toned down. Zandra Rhodes' Conceptual Chic collection in 1978, for example, featured a softer version of the pins, rips and spikes of street-style punk. The revolutionary Vivienne Westwood was not one to hold back, however, and her T-shirts depicting a less than respectful image of the Queen started a trend that ran riot down London's fashionable King's Road. For these collections, jewellery in the traditional sense was abandoned and replaced by embroidered rips, polished safety pins and studded fetish cuffs as symbols of alienation.

Despite the anti-capitalist campaign of the young, high street, high fashion and high society jewellery continued to enjoy their individual styles in nine-carat gold and silver, eighteen-carat gold and bright, large gems or diamonds and platinum. The more feminine era of Art Nouveau was also revisited by fashion and jewellery designers alike resulting in long, flowing garments, and jewellery to match. The jewels tended to incorporate the most typical Art Nouveau images – above all scrolling flowers and female figures with flowing hair – and they were generally mass-produced and poorly made by machine. The influence of other cultures can also be seen in jewellery with the popularity of large beads of African and Indian origin, which were combined with copper and silver hand-wrought ornaments and strung together to form huge necklaces. Symbolic pieces in silver and turquoise made by native American Indians were also popular. The 1960s and 1970s saw a return of the influence of Hollywood on design, together with the newer influence of television, as the 1920s and 1940s styles seen in films such as *Bonnie and Clyde* (1967), *The Great Gatsby* (1974) and *Annie Hall* (1977) promoted period revivals, while popular television series such as *The Avengers* and *Charlie's Angels* carried Hollywood glitz and style around the world.

The end of the 1970s witnessed a fitness craze and the resulting female figure ideal, super-fit and supple, was shown off in leotards and Lycra, and adorned at the disco in sequins and brightly coloured costume jewellery. The influence of nightclubbing also spawned other looks. In New York's Club Studio 54 the new party animal was portrayed as elegant and chic in American designer Halston's 1975 collection, launched at the club. Up-to-the-minute jewellery for clubbing featured computer-technology designs in metal and coloured plastic by the Austrian Fritz Maierhofer and the Englishman Roger Morris, or space-technology materials such as titanium and niobium, successfully worked by Edward de Large in the United States. In The Blitz nightclub, in London, a whole different style was emerging. This was the "New Romantic" style, characterized by the white cotton frills of the pirate costume, which gained widespread popularity. Teamed with gold bows, tassels and fringes, it gave a relieved public a strong contrast to the stark designs of punk.

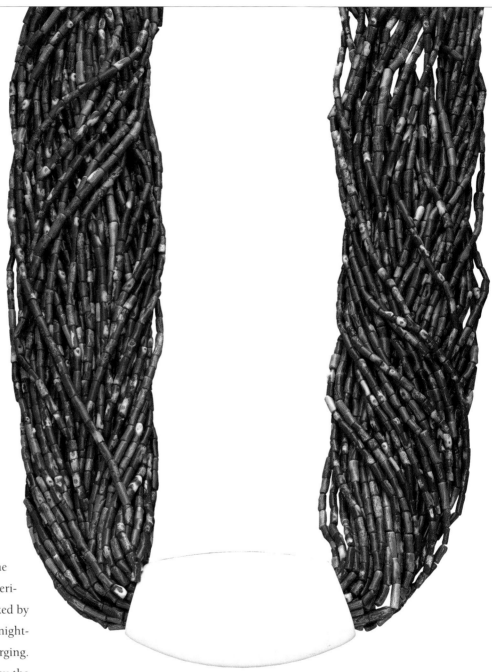

above: *This ethnic-influenced necklace by Angela Pintaldi is made from strands of coral with a large cylinder of ivorine, an ivory simulant, c. 1970.*

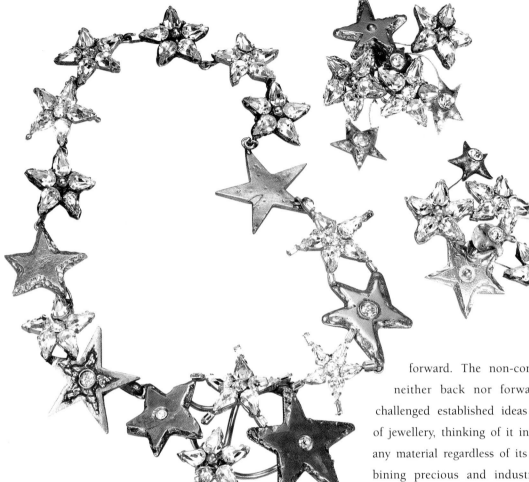

above: *This gilt metal and paste suite is from Chanel and would certainly shine on the dance floor.*

far right: *A suite of eighteen-carat gold and diamond jewellery by Kutchinsky c. 1970.*

Alongside the evolution of the traditional jewel in "street" fashion and in mainstream jewellery, a small and slowly growing movement of non-conformist designer jewellers was being established during the 1970s. Changes had already been seen in the work of commercial mainstream jewellers, such as Bulgari, who looked back to the past for inspiration, and in the work of innovative new mainstream jewellers, such as Andrew Grima, who looked

forward. The non-conformist jewellers looked neither back nor forward but elsewhere. They challenged established ideas about the very meaning of jewellery, thinking of it in terms of body art. Using any material regardless of its intrinsic value, and combining precious and industrial metals, they created individual pieces that demanded – and still demand – effort to be worn and that have therefore never been popular with the general jewellery-wearing population.

Accepted innovative mainstream design and non-conformist design are perhaps best bridged by the easily wearable jewellery of Austrian-born British artist Gerda Flockinger (b. 1927), whose molten-looking, fused, blistered and bubbled gold with inset gems has an almost accidentally organic appearance that she created by ignoring the accepted confines of goldsmithing. Flockinger established an experimental course in jewellery at Hornsey College of Art in London in 1962

right: *A Gerda Flockinger pendant necklace, the textured, coiled and worked-on tubular sections combined with part-worked amethyst, turquoise and cultured pearls. The necklace was created in 1965 and the detachable pendant in 1971.*

for Artist Jewellers whose goals diverged from the traditional. The course encouraged a pioneering approach to studio jewellery, and fostered innovative ideas and experimental techniques. She taught many of the new emerging non-conformist talents, including David Poston (b. 1948), who caused a stir when he produced a necklace for an elephant, and Charlotte de Syllas (b. 1946) who combines months of detailed craftsmanship with a range of decorative materials to create unique jewels.

The Netherlands in particular experienced an inventive period in jewellery design from the mid-1960s through to the 1970s. One group of non-conformist jewellers who all wanted to revolt against their traditional training and break with the past banded together to form the "B.O.E." or "Bond van obloerege eddelsmeden", which translates as "jewellers in revolt". Emmy van Leersum (1930–84) and Gijs Bakker (b. 1942) were the main exponents of this ethic. They experimented with a number of new materials, and aluminium became one of their favourites as its light weight was perfect for forming large pieces. When they exhibited with others at Eindhoven in 1969 a common principle seemed to be emerging, one that saw the body as an important part of the jewel and not just the thing on which the jewel was hung. They might produce, for example, not an earring but an ear-piece, a shaped metal form that enveloped the lower portion of the ear. Yet things continued to move fast, and even as many Dutch jewellers began to adopt this principle, others began a further revolt against this somewhat clinical approach and looked towards Britain where jewellery design was looser and freer. Indeed, during the 1970s an important exchange of ideas between many Dutch and British jewellers had a strong influence on the use of textiles and colour in the Netherlands.

Non-conformist jewellery is exciting, stimulating and controversial, ideal for display in galleries, exhibitions and museums, but the pieces are basically works of art for the body rather than jewellery in the accepted sense. A gap still existed between mainstream jewellery and non-conformist works in the 1970s and during that decade and the 1980s this was filled by an international group who came to be known as Contemporary Jewellers. They provided discerning clients with original jewels and their ranks included Wendy Ramshaw and David Watkins in England, James Bennett and Arline M. Fisch in the United States, Yasuki Hiramatsu in Japan and Bruno Martinazzi in Italy. These craftspeople, and many others working from individual design studios, produced single pieces on commission or variations on an established theme. The jewels were often sculptural or, as with Wendy Ramshaw, could be incorporated into a sculpture but were still intended, first and foremost, to be pieces of jewellery.

The main ethics that influenced the Contemporary Jeweller at this time were that their jewellery should be: fresh and avoid the use of cliché in design; exciting, robust and cheap; able to be worn by either sex; against vulgarity and status-seeking; and able to work with and complement the wearer's body. These aims could be achieved by jewellers who chose to work in non-precious materials, either for reasons of economy or to break with the values of wealth, status and power that were associated with gem-encrusted jewels; or by those who purposely embraced the traditional materials but focused on them in a new way.

Wendy Ramshaw was an important figure in 1970s jewellery design. A leading exponent of precious-metal jewellery, she also experimented with other materials and is famous for her ring sets, which combine jewellery and

left: *A good example of one of Wendy Ramshaw's ring sets, dating from 1971. The steel stand is inlaid with resin bands and the gold rings are set with turquoise. These rings can be removed and worn singly or together in various combinations.*

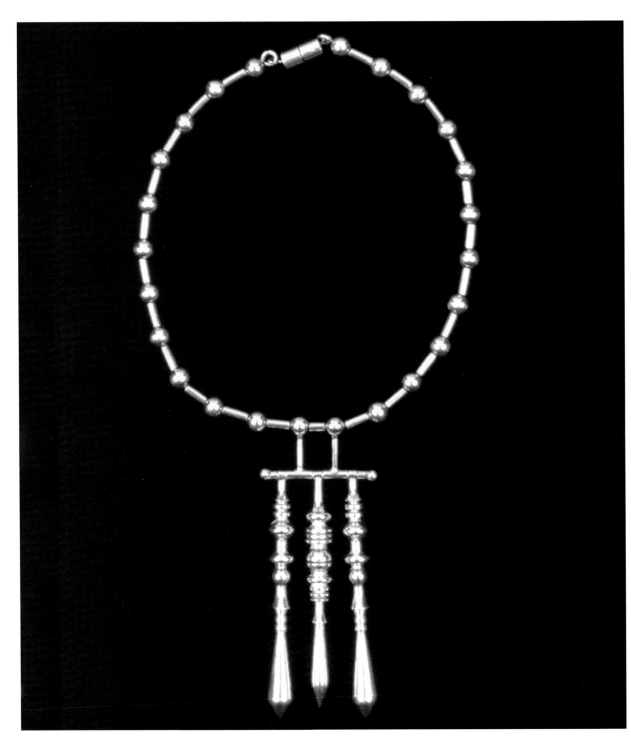

right: *A bead and cylinder silver necklace by Wendy Ramshaw, dating from 1972.*

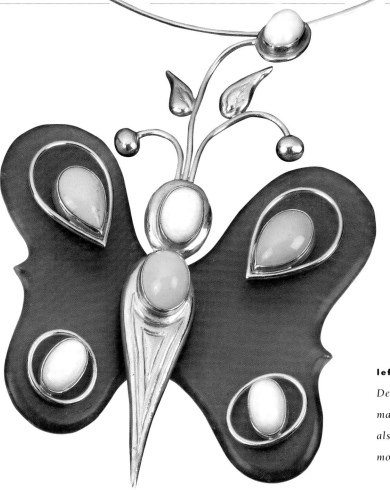

left: *A butterfly necklace by Greek designer Depy Chandris, from 1970. It incorporates a man-made material similar to acrylic, but is also set with turquoise and coral with gold mounts and collar.*

sculpture in one, and utilize Perspex, steel, silver, gold and gems to provide a sculpture that doubles as a storage facility for her jewellery. She is widely believed to have been one of the first to design pieces that both decorated the human body and could stand alone as decorative objects. A recent series of her work was inspired by Picasso's portrayals of women, and interprets the colour, line, shape and volume of the female subjects in his paintings as sculptural jewels. Her jewellery has been the subject of several exhibitions and her works are represented in many major institutions as fine examples of material, form and ornament combined.

Another leading British Contemporary Jeweller, David Watkins, utilized his training as a sculptor to produce large, non-conformist body-fitting neck-pieces and bracelets in the 1970s, before developing contemporary jewellery that involved highly coloured, neoprene-coated pieces made of steel. It is in his work that we can best see the deliberate avoidance of fastenings, clips and chains, which were becoming so important in the work of many designers. His jewellery has often been exhibited, especially in the latter part of the twentieth century, and many galleries and museums worldwide feature his pieces in their collections.

A DIAMOND IS FOREVER

"A diamond is forever", one of the most enduring advertising slogans of all time, was part of an advertising campaign launched in 1948 on behalf of jewellery retailers by De Beers to promote the sale of diamonds to the romantic market, notably for engagements, births and anniversaries.

De Beers Consolidated Mines Ltd was formed in 1889 by the amalgamation of Barnarto Mining and Cecil Rhodes De Beers Mining. The resulting group controlled the five big newly developed diamond mines in South Africa and thus ensured a supply of diamonds to the world market throughout the twentieth century. As the geology of the volcanic outlet pipes, which carried diamond crystals towards the surface from their formation point twenty kilometres (about twelve miles) below, became better understood and prospecting methods improved, more diamond mines were discovered in Africa. De Beers acquired a controlling interest in these mines, and many others – indeed, they soon controlled such a large proportion of the world's mines that they were in a position to command the world market by regulating the supply of rough diamonds to the cutters. The increased availability of diamonds in the late nineteenth and early twentieth centuries meant that these stones were now more readily available to more consumers, and were no longer restricted to the aristocracy. However, by controlling the numbers released, De Beers ensured that the market was never flooded and diamonds were, and still are, perceived as luxury items with investment potential.

Victorian diamond-cutters used a version of the brilliant cut that included fifty-eight facets, based on the principles of preserving as much of the weight of the original crystal as possible and having a gem that reacted well to the available light source, which, at the turn of the twentieth century, was the incandescent light from gas mantles and candles. Upon hitting the deep prism sides of the old-cut stones it gave wonderful displays of spectral colours, flashes of red, blue and yellow. This play of light was enhanced by the popular practice of mounting the gems *en tremblant*, the sprung

①

1 This deep cushion-shaped stone is an example of an old-brilliant-cut diamond; a more modern cut is seen to the left.
2 One of the winners of the De Beers Diamond International Awards in 1998, this bangle is set with the modern princess-cut stones and was made by Oliver Passetto.
3 This diamond yacht brooch incorporates a number of fancy cutting styles.
4 Three diamond rings of significance – one colourless, another of a peach colour, and the third an important intense blue drop-cut.

❷

triangular cut, also rose in popularity, later followed by an interesting array of specially designed and named new cuts at the end of the twentieth century.

Always looking for ways to encourage more creativity in diamond jewellery, De Beers established an annual international competition in 1955: the Diamond International Awards. These rewarded original design and material that combined beauty, harmony and function. The award of several prizes allowed a competitor to become a member of the Diamond International Academy, joining such names as Pierre Sterlé, Jean Schlumberger and Seaman Schepps.

❸

The De Beers advertising campaign was also responsible for the suggestion that an engagement ring should be of a value equivalent to two months of the proposer's salary. Further advertising was targeted to fit in with supply – solitaires were pushed if they were plentiful, and clusters were heavily advertised during periods when mainly small stones were produced.

settings allowing the maximum play of light as the jewel moved. With the growing prevalence of electric light and the emergence of the platinum-mounted Garland Style, which required a white effect (see page 38), there was considerable research into the cutting of diamonds. In 1919, theoretical mathematician Marcel Tolkowsky published his design for the proportions of a diamond cut to achieve maximum brilliancy (the return to the eye of white light), combined with an optimum degree of dispersion (the breaking up of the light into spectral colours); and a slightly modified version of this modern brilliant cut was generally adopted.

Another development in cutting resulted in the baguette diamond, which became popular in the Art Deco period (see chapter two), the rectangular stone lending itself well to the geometric shapes of Art Deco style. More stones can be produced using this shallow cut as the baguette does not require a deep crystal. Other fancy cuts, including a

The 1950s were a time of discovery in the USSR, and important diamond pipe mines proved to be rich sources of material, although difficult to mine through the permafrost. In 1960, De Beers agreed to purchase all the gem rough that the Soviets wished to export to the West. At this point the strain of controlling the world market by buying the increasing production from around the world and stockpiling material in times of economic difficulty put the company under huge economic pressure. However, the established system of a few invited buyers being allowed to purchase controlled parcels or "sights" of rough diamond, which they then distributed to the cutters, held the market

❹

together, avoiding a sudden flood of cheap diamonds and maintaining the public belief in the inherent value of the gems.

Public appreciation of diamonds continued to rise through to the 1980s when sales of significant diamonds hit the headlines. Historically, the general understanding had been that the whiter the diamond the better, but in October 1987 a fancy purplish-red diamond weighing 0.95 carats was sold in auction for just under one million dollars. This sale also coincided with the appearance on the market of pink diamonds from the Argyle Mines of Kimberley, Western Australia. This mine, discovered in 1979, is now one of the largest producers of diamonds in the world, although the majority of its production is for industrial use. Around five per cent of the stones mined are, however, of gem quality, and this includes a small quantity of rare pink stones. All the mine's production is marketed through Argyle diamond sales, bypassing De Beers, the pinks being sold by tender and by public auction.

Other sales show the strength of the demand for important coloured gems. A fancy blue drop-cut diamond of 42.92 carats (previously the property of Mikhail Terestchenko, the Russian Minister of Foreign Affairs in 1917) was sold to a Saudi Arabian dealer in 1984 for ten million Swiss francs (nearly half a million US dollars). It was described as being similar to the famous Hope diamond, which had been donated to the Smithsonian Institution in Washington, D.C. by the great diamond dealer Harry Winston in 1958. In 1988,

a giant, fancy, brownish-yellow brilliant-cut gem of 407 carats and internally flawless was sold in New York for $15,200,000. The demand for spectacular stones, particularly from certain collectors from Middle Eastern countries, altered the market significantly, so that large crystals, which would previously have been cut into several stones, were now cut as one. By 1990, these specialized buyers began to realize that the very rarity of the great stones they already owned was at risk, and they withdrew from the market.

The discovery of large diamond deposits in Canada, which remained outside the De Beers cartel, and the reduced control of Russian output, finally led De Beers to change course and join the major diamond dealer Lazar Kaplan in marketing directly to the public.

In 2000, public opinion was aroused against the purchase of diamonds from Angola when it emerged that the proceeds of diamond sales were funding the war there. Traditionally all diamonds handled by the Central Selling Organization arm of De Beers had been sorted and graded in London without regard to their origin, but now new systems of tracking are needed to ensure that diamonds can be sold as being free from the taint of funding a war. Canadian diamonds, mined, cut and marketed under direct control of the specific mining company, have adopted a laser-inscribed polar bear on the edge of the diamond, and this form of branding is now being followed by several retailers to establish an identity for their stones.

Some retailers are branding their diamonds by developing new patented cutting styles and many diamonds are now accompanied by a certificate giving details of their origin and quality. These certificates will detail the important information that dictates the value of the stone, known as the four Cs (see page 185): cut, colour, clarity and carat weight. The cut will describe the shape of the stone but, more importantly, will determine the quality of the cutting and the correct proportions for that cut. The "colour" of colourless or white diamonds is most often assessed by the international scale set by the Gemological Institute of America. The best score on the scale is D, and it then descends alphabetically with the minute changes in colour. The border between G and H is the area where the first tiny hint of yellow can be seen, and as the scale progresses the tints become stronger. These grades are decided upon with the aid of a set of master stones. The clarity of a stone is dependent upon the number, size and colour of inclusions within the stone and on its surface, when viewed under 10x magnification. Stones vary from the flawless specimens down to the obviously spotty or piqué stones, with

5 This pink diamond is the drop of a diamond and coloured diamond brooch; pinks are very popular and can command high prices but the rarest and most expensive is red.

6 This "chameleon" diamond changes colour under different conditions. The yellowish green temporarily turns to vivid yellow when it is heated or left in the dark.

7 This exceptional top-quality D-colour diamond is flawless.

8 Although most inclusions in diamonds devalue the stone, the unusual can increase it; this cube-shaped diamond exhibits a cloudy inclusion that forms a Maltese Cross.

❽

VVS (very, very small inclusion), VS (very small inclusion) and SI (slight inclusion) between the two extremes.

Carat weight is measured in a metric standard: one carat equals 200 milligrams or one-fifth of a metric gram. A carat is divided into 100 points, so half a carat may also be referred to as 50 points. As the modern brilliant is cut to a mathematical formula, rough estimates of weight may be made without removing the stone from the mount; this is achieved using a metal or plastic gauge with holes cut to the same size as the correlating size and weight of a diamond. More accurate sizes can be assessed using the "leveridge" gauge, where measurements of width and depth can be cross-referenced and a weight arrived at by using a table designed for this purpose. Carat weight is an important factor in the valuation of a stone, but bigger is not always better. This only applies if all the other Cs are good; otherwise it may be better to have a small perfect stone than a large imperfect one.

chapter five

POWER AND ROMANCE
the 1980s and 1990s

THE 1980S

In the 1980s, the world of fashion was influenced by two rather contrasting styles: the romantic look, characterized by Lady Diana Spencer, who was to become the Princess of Wales; and "power dressing". Power dressing was epitomized by the shoulder-padded costumes of the female characters in the enormously popular American soap operas *Dallas* and *Dynasty*, whose fictional success mirrored the true-life emergence of women in top business positions during a strong economic boom. It was a fashion that reflected a desire to present a powerful and strong image signifying that the women who wore these clothes were in charge of their lives, and jewellery became huge and glossy to match it. Small and delicate was "out". If you had money you were expected to flaunt it, and loud and gaudy, large and obvious became the required day and evening wear. Although these fast-changing fashions were mostly accommodated by inexpensive jewels or cheap costume jewellery, they did still have an impact on the more expensive pieces.

Another method of flaunting wealth and power was the ostentatious display of designer labels and "branding". Suddenly what you wore was not nearly as important as who made it. Labels once neatly tucked away within garment interiors were now sewn to be seen; and the designer's name was evident on jeans, in house logos used as embroidered motifs, incorporated into the design of the material or brazenly worn on buttons.

Many of the major fashion houses produced jewellery and costume jewellery to complete their "look", and this had to keep up with the branding trend. French fashion house Chanel had a new director, Karl Lagerfeld, who was taken on in 1983 to modernize the firm after the period of style stagnation that had followed the death of Coco Chanel in 1971. Jewellery was an essential part of Lagerfeld's relaunched look, and was characterized by the bold use of an exaggerated version of the double "C" logo and multiversions of Chanel's signature

left: *This Seaman Schepps chunky necklace is made from gold and various woods, and probably dates from the 1980s. It incorporates two clasps that can be taken apart, allowing it to be worn as two bracelets.*

gilt chains. At the same time, the Italian design house Gucci launched a chain style from an existing design reminiscent of the marine or anchor link and made it recognizably their own.

Alongside this craze for displaying wealth and power was a demand for a softer, more natural look. This was heightened by the arrival in British public life of Lady Diana Spencer, who took the world by storm when she became engaged to Prince Charles. Her wide-eyed shyness captured many hearts during her astonishing progression from teenage nursery worker to fairy-tale princess. The world was gripped by the royal romance and by the wedding in 1981, and all eyes were on the new Diana, Princess of Wales; indeed, she soon became the most photographed woman in the world. Her sapphire and diamond oval-cluster engagement ring pushed the sales of similar styles through the roof, and she gave the single row of uniform pearls a huge boost worldwide, giving it an importance as an accessory for both day and evening wear that was to continue through to the next century.

The mid-1980s saw an introduction of more relaxed, less structured clothes. American designer Donna Karan's 1985 collection promoted "clothes that would travel, interchange and impress". Her simple designs were enlivened by the addition of gold-plated jewellery by the American jeweller Robert Lee Morris whose jewels of elegant simplicity provided a dramatic change from the over-ornate boldness of power jewellery. This idea of designing jewellery with clothes to provide a total look rather than merely a decorative feature was taken up and enhanced by French designer Christian Lacroix, whose lush, colourful designs were particularly attractive to younger customers. His clothes were complemented by his oversized and exaggerated costume jewels, including his fabulous trademark cross pendants. Along with his love of bold colour and puffball skirts he not only created a complete antithesis of the more mature look provided by Donna Karan and Robert Lee Morris, but the confusion of fabric, colour and texture provided a very different look from the orderly ferociousness of power dressing.

Those craving a sense of opulence and selectivity were catered for by the impressive new and most unusual works of jeweller Joe Arthur Rosenthal. He has been widely acknowledged as the inheritor of the mantle of Fabergé and Lalique (see chapter one), being the creator of intricately detailed and unusual jewels in unique settings. He and his partner Pierre Jeannet use unusual gemstones in stunning colour combinations to provide a distinctive personal style. In November 1987, in celebration of the

left: *The twin "C" logo of Chanel, evident in the buckle of this silver belt, illustrates the 1980s fashion for the designer label.*

below: *A pair of sapphire and green tourmaline earrings by JAR, examples of the new palette of colours and styles.*

left: *A fine lavender jadeite bangle, certificated as natural colour and no polymer detected.*

right: *A charming jadeite and diamond brooch modelled as a Siamese cat, the body and head of translucent vivid emerald-green jadeite.*

tenth anniversary of the opening of his Paris boutique, discreetly identified by the initials "JAR", Rosenthal held an exhibition of his work at the National Academy of Design in New York. This started a slow but decided change in jewellery design. His works take months or years to complete and so are comparatively rare and very costly, but they gradually came to the attention of, and were worn by, the very wealthy and members of the top echelons of society, eventually inspiring others to adopt similarly unusual colours and styles. This gradual adoption of a wider colour range and unusual gems such as blue tourmaline and green garnet has spread to lower-value jewels by other jewellers and manufacturers, providing a level of elegant and affordable pieces that would not exist without Rosenthal's inspiration.

The boost to the economies of Asia provided by the flood of international companies taking advantage of a willing and economic local workforce provided new wealth in the 1980s, and with it new opportunities for jewellery sales in Southeast Asia. The Asian passion for emerald-green and lavender jade, much of it superbly carved, soon spread across the world, although the centre for jade was, and still is, Hong Kong. Modern designs of diamonds and yellow gold were also popular with the fashion-conscious Southeast Asian women of this period, and only brand-new pieces would do. Coloured diamonds, originally popularized in New York, now spread to the region and became highly prized. Designs of flora and fauna were popular and were epitomized by the work of Sammy Chow, a director of the pearl company Trio, in Hong Kong; and Bulgari who opened stores in Tokyo, Osaka, Hong Kong and Singapore in the second half of the 1980s.

The Chinese improved their production of cultured pearls, and numbers on the wholesale market increased dramatically. The desire for bigger pearls had also increased, so the farms in the South Seas that specialize in the larger sizes – those over nine millimetres (0.35 inches) – produced more to meet this most welcome demand. Unfortunately, some standards were lowered to facilitate this, and many South Sea cultured pearls, although cheaper, are now of poor quality.

THE 1990S

The 1990s saw the demise of the ever-younger supermodel and fashion was no longer ruled by the young, as it had been since the power suit faded from the scene, although a separate youth culture was still strong.

right: *Each pearl in this good quality cultured pearl necklace, with a diamond cluster clasp, is approximately 11–14mm in diameter, shown here with a pair of similarly styled earrings.*

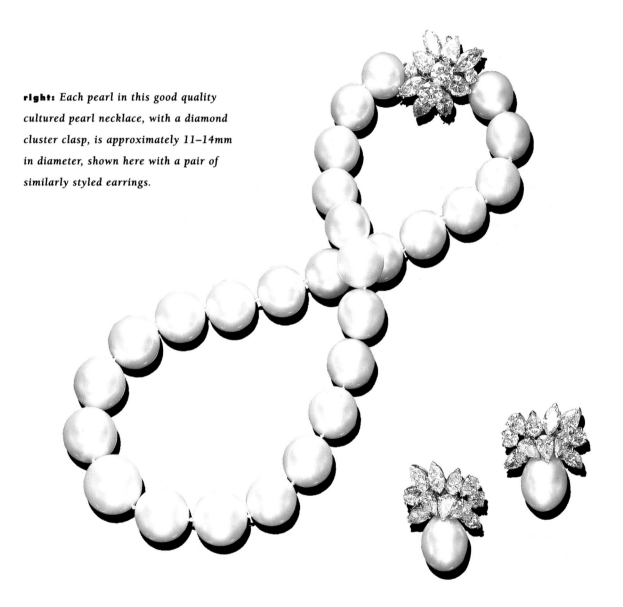

right: *The ring on the right is by the German firm Neissing and is an example of a tension set diamond. The other ring is a traditional gypsy set band.*

The baby boomers had matured and so had fashion. The mature woman was back in the public eye. Indeed, Italian actress and model Isabella Rossellini signed a new contract with the cosmetics firm Lancôme at the age of thirty-nine. Princess Diana, reaching her thirties and divorced in this decade, could indulge her desire to wear what she wanted; she turned to Chanel, Lacroix and Versace, and wore lower necklines, shorter skirts and higher heels. The power suits and branding had disappeared along with the shoulder pad and the Chanel button; a brief flirtation with the 1970s saw the return of the flared trouser; and accessories became softer and less aggressive. Fashion styling still depicted women as "in charge" and stronger than ever, but the new image was more subtle. Jewellery followed suit, realizing a more simple and sophisticated look typified by the diamond single-stone pendant or small plain cross suspended at the base of the neck by a delicate chain. Cheaper equivalent styles were achieved with the use of diamond simulants such as cubic zirconia, often "suspended in air" (strung on a nylon thread).

Towards the end of the decade, Japanese designers led the return to the white look in jewellery. Platinum was the metal of choice, and was accompanied by new cuts and settings for stones. The tension-set diamond, developed by the German firm Neissing, probably epitomizes the last new style of the century. The stone is unsupported, held in place by the shoulders squeezing from either side. It takes a tough stone to withstand this pressure, and so the diamond is really the best one to take the strain. Thus we see jewellery styles at the end of the century mirroring the fashion of its opening years, with the white of platinum and diamond as its strongest theme.

left: *Influenced by the earlier Surrealist movement, this necklace of jasper, rock crystal, diamond and tourmaline by Chaumet is a superb piece of sculptural art from the 1970s.*

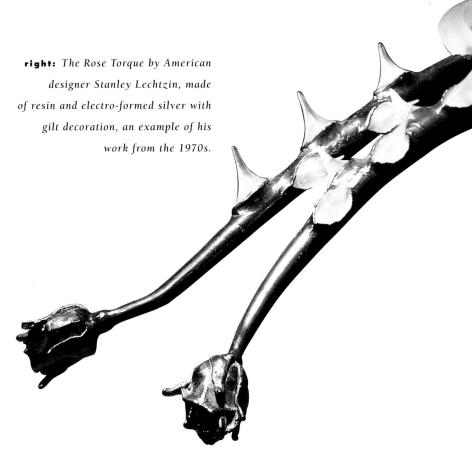

right: *The Rose Torque by American designer Stanley Lechtzin, made of resin and electro-formed silver with gilt decoration, an example of his work from the 1970s.*

THE ARTIST JEWELLER AND THE CONTEMPORARY JEWELLER

Alongside mainstream jewellers were Contemporary Jewellers, who diverged from traditional styles and used an ever-expanding range of untraditional materials. As a result, they were closely involved with the fast-moving fashion industry, and thus commercial in approach, but at the same time, during the last segment of the twentieth century the concept of "Art Jewellery" was emerging fully into the commercial world. One might ask what

the difference between the work of the Artist Jeweller and that of the Contemporary Jeweller is, and indeed there appears to be a very fine line between them. Sometimes an artist may be described as a Contemporary Jeweller in one publication and as an Artist Jeweller in another, with Americans more commonly using the Artist Jeweller description. The premise seems to be that Art Jewellery is first and foremost a sculpture, a piece of art, and the fact that it might be worn, often precariously, on the body as a piece of jewellery is only of secondary importance. It is a kind of public art, displayed in a moving exhibition, and by definition should be a one-of-a-kind piece and not produced in any sort of number (although a few artists allowed limited editions of some pieces to be made). Perhaps most importantly, it should be both designed and made by the artist. In contrast, the term "Contemporary Jewellery" is often used to describe jewellery that may be similar in style to some Art Jewellery, but may be mass-produced and have a more commercial bias in addition to its artistic merits, allowing it to reach more people.

right: *Organic jewels and objets d'art by the American artist John Hatleberg, from 2000. The cobs have applied pearl "corn" and the "pearl pods" have a gold wire vine to which the pods can be attached for use as a necklace.*

right: *A group of diamond-set, fabulously carved snails by Russian artist Slava Tulupov, including chalcedony, smokey quartz and black jade, all from the late 1990s. The central piece is an award-winning sculpture but the smaller three are stick pins.*

The concept of Art Jewellery was not entirely new – Lalique had been producing unusual one-of-a-kind pieces of art, that were not necessarily designed to be worn, at the beginning of the century. However, the modern interpretation of the term – as more futuristic designs distinct from current trends – found some of its earliest influences in the work of the American Earl Pardon and the Castillo brothers who worked in Taxco, Mexico, in the 1940s and 1950s, together with a landmark exhibition entitled "Modern Handmade Jewellery" held in New York's Museum of Modern Art in 1946. The exhibition brought together jewellery by artists and sculptors such as Alexander Calder and Jacques Lipschitz, and pieces by jewellers including Margaret de Patta and Sam Kramer. It was the first exhibition to exhibit and acknowledge jewellery by prominent sculptors, with sculptural pieces by jewellers whose work moved away from the traditional, to be known as wearable art. Other exhibitions followed, and in 1968 a group of artists established the Society of North American Goldsmiths to further the aims of, and encourage, other Artist Jewellers in the United States.

As with the Contemporary Jewellers, the material used by Artist Jewellers is important not for its intrinsic value but as a medium to realize the artist's vision. Thus in the United States Robert Ebendorf (b. 1938), one of the founding members of the Society of North American Goldsmiths, has from the 1980s onwards won acclaim for his collage techniques, which incorporate anything from paper through to broken glass; and Marjorie Schick (b. 1941) produces papier-mâché mini-sculptures in bright colours, which she calls "paintings to wear". Mary Lee Hu (b. 1943) uses a basketry technique to weave collars and bangles in gold; while Arline Fisch (b. 1931) uses textile techniques of weaving and knitting to produce large collars, armlets and

body pieces, mostly in silver and gold. Another founder member of the Society of North American Goldsmiths, Stanley Lechtzin (b. 1936), has become an acknowledged master of electroforming – a technique in which metal is electrolytically deposited on to a conductive matrix – and he also uses plastics to great effect.

In 1996, a group similar to the Society of North American Goldsmiths was formed: the Gem Artists of North America. Like their goldsmith colleagues, they are devoted to the concept of the individual jewel, but their greatest interest lies in how the gem is used. They are passionate about how each precious or "semi-precious" gem is cut, carved and mounted, ranging from tiny jewels to large sculptural

above: *This perfume bottle by Michael Christie and Susan Allan has parts that are detachable for use as jewellery.*

pieces. Amongst this group is John Hatleberg, who has worked with De Beers and top natural history museums around the world to create exact replicas of famous diamonds. He creates fabulous stands of mica and resin to enhance his jewellery when not worn, and has produced fascinating *objets d'art* including his well-received corn cobs. Made using the natural cob and applying pearl "corn", these have been bought by royalty and celebrities worldwide, and much of his work is included in collections or exhibitions in both the United States and Britain.

Another member is Russian artist Slava Tulupov. Born in St Petersburg, he spent his youth and university years near the Hermitage Museum where he was a frequent visitor, becoming strongly influenced by the work of Fabergé. This influence is now clearly seen in his carvings. He moved to the United States from the oppressive atmosphere in Russia in 1991, and was recognized by the American government as an artist with extraordinary abilities. It is these abilities that have won him several awards and the praise of many connoisseurs of fine work.

Other notable members of the Gem Artists of North America include Michael Christie, who specializes in multifunctional perfume bottles that provide decorative housing for jewellery. The stopper doubles as a pendant, and the decorative feature stones may be removed from the bottle stand and worn as earrings. Some of his pieces incorporate intricate carvings by Susan Allen deep within the crystal body of the bottle.

Allen was originally a painter and turned to the established art of reverse crystal carving to depict her pictures; a complicated scene can take her many months to complete. Working in topaz, aquamarine or quartz, she uses the natural elements of the stone as part of the composition – moss-like inclusions of dendrite turn to seaweed, golden rods of rutile provide a hiding place for fish and tiny villages spring from crystalline hillsides.

In Europe, the modern Artist or Contemporary Jeweller also experimented with new materials or different ways of using established favourites. The artist sculptor César Baldaccini was inspired by the disruption of World War Two and its images of distorted metal, and by the introduction of a new press for scrap-metal cars, to develop his Nouveau Realisme ideas into "Compressions". He used colourful cubes of compressed cars and various scrap materials in his sculpture, and went on to develop "Jewellery Compressions" in 1971 when he was asked by a friend to convert a box of jewellery into a single pendant. He compressed the contents into a fascinating single jewel of multiple precious components, the start of a series of such pieces.

The British artist Catherine Martin studied music at the Guildhall School of Music in London and then the Franz Liszt Music Academy in Budapest, Hungary, before travelling to Japan where she learnt the art of silk braiding at the Domyo School of Kumihimo. Using traditional silks, she has provided braid for works by Charlotte de Syllus, but has now turned her braiding skills to precious metals. She has won many awards for these jewels and has exhibited in both the United States and Britain. Examples

above: *A compression pendant by sculptor César Baldaccini revealing some of the crushed components.*

far right: *An intricately braided gold wire necklace by the acclaimed British artist Catherine Martin, c. 2000.*

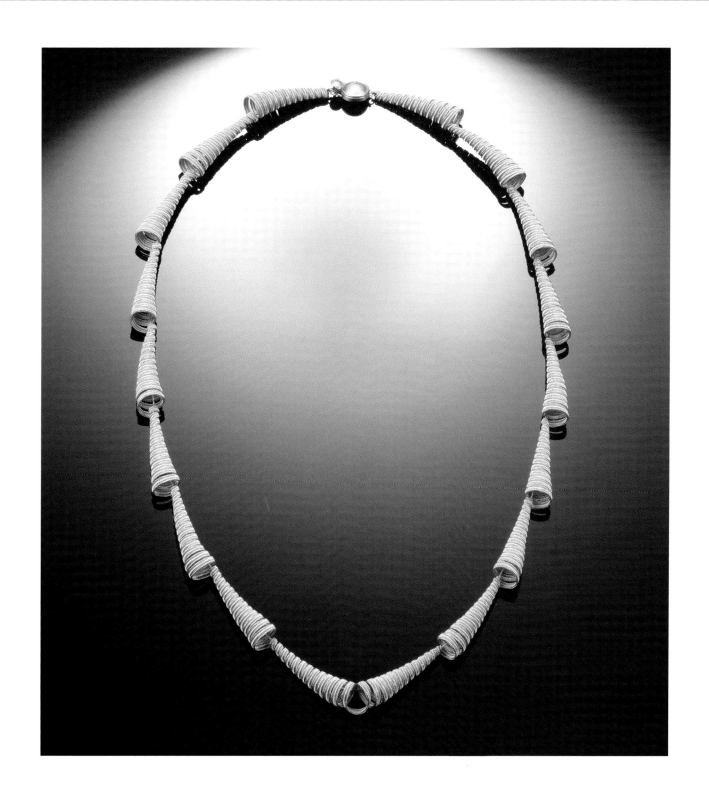

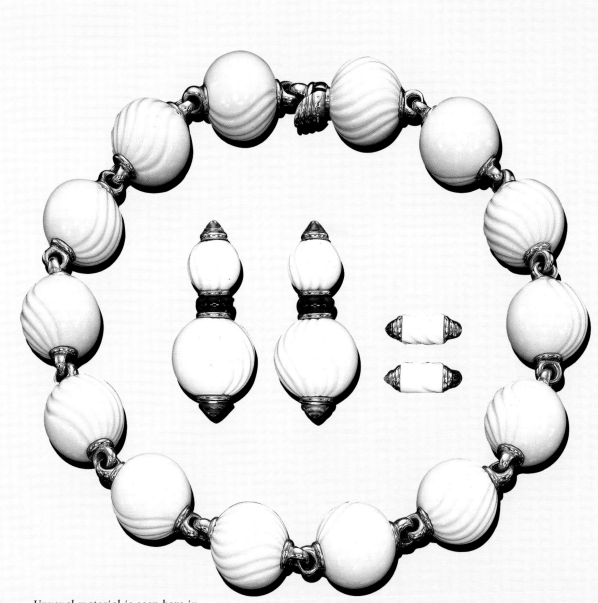

above: *Unusual material is seen here in this Bulgari porcelain and gold "Chandra" necklace from 1994.*

of her work are held in various British museums and collections, including the Victoria and Albert Museum in London. Music is still an important part of her life, as she listens to Bach while working.

Peter Chang, another British artist, originally trained in model-making and fine art in the 1960s. This influence is obvious in his colourful, highly ornate and intriguing designs constructed mainly of acrylic, polyester and lacquer. His work has been exhibited or included in collections in Europe and the United States, and has been featured on the catwalk in top fashion shows where his unconventional sculptural designs work well.

Other exciting new discoveries in materials for jewellery included titanium, a "refractory" metal capable of changing its surface until it reflects every colour of the rainbow. This is achieved when it is exposed to a specific electrolytic solution. The use of titanium started in the 1970s and peaked in the 1980s – one of the first to use it was the Scottish Artist Jeweller Ann Marie Shillito – but it is a difficult metal to work with and few jewellers have continued to use it to any great effect.

A slight move away from unusual materials can be seen in the changing mediums employed by the Dutch jeweller Robert Smit. His 1970s work incorporated the use of acrylic and computer-programming components. However, when after a short respite from jewellery production he returned in the 1980s, he used different coloured golds produced by the addition of various alloys. His contemporaries criticized him for re-establishing jewellery as a status symbol. However, his strongest critic at the time, Gijs Bakker, later incorporated gold and diamonds in his own work – although these materials sometimes feature alongside less orthodox elements, as in pieces that use PVC as the setting for diamonds.

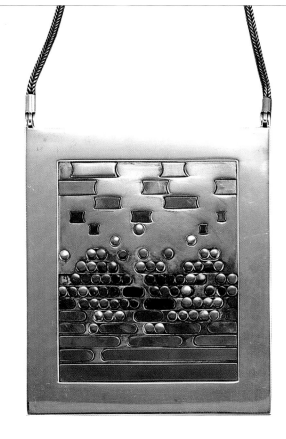

There is still a light-hearted approach in many contemporary works that may be classified as Art or Contemporary Jewellery. These are often inspired by now-established artists such as the British jeweller and sculptor Andrew Logan. Logan's pieces are bizarre and yet still glamorous, often with mirror fragments and glitter set into resin with simple safety-pin fastenings. Some might term this type of jewellery "costume jewellery" as it appears to be of cheap manufacture and is composed of inexpensive materials. However, as many of the pieces that we have been describing are individual pieces and not duplicated by mass production, they should perhaps more accurately be termed "Art Jewels".

above: *Vari-coloured titanium segments produce a new effect in this pendant necklace made by Julia Whitman, an example from the mid-1970s.*

COSTUME JEWELLERY

The continuous search for, and use of, new materials and designs has brought the work of Contemporary Jewellers, Art Jewellers and manufacturers of costume jewellery together at various levels, catering for the huge appetite of a scattered class system with vastly different ideals as well as variable financial resources. Contemporary Jewellers cater for the client who wishes to update her jewellery wardrobe without straying too far from accepted ideals and traditions. Artist Jewellers, on the other hand, provide pieces that may appeal to those customers who can afford a possibly expensive one-of-a-kind work that may be difficult to wear but that nonetheless commands attention – and has the advantage of possibly providing a long-term investment.

left: High manufacturing standards can be seen in this highly flexible bracelet set with calibre rubies with diamond trim, by Aletto Brothers.

The world of costume jewellery can and does overlap these areas (it is often difficult to classify some works); it also feeds the desire for new and interesting pieces in a fast-moving and hungry market at the lower price level. Many of the new materials available to manufacturers in the latter part of the century enabled increasingly futuristic designs to be realized. Suddenly all materials and methods of manufacture became acceptable, and indeed their use was encouraged by the desire to produce something totally different and, in many people's eyes, rebellious. Costume jewellery has contributed greatly to the jewellery of the twentieth century, both in shadowing the fashions in precious jewels and bringing these fashions to a wider audience, and in the general use and acceptance of different, often much cheaper, materials in the composition of new jewels.

above left: *Bordering art and costume jewellery, this 1981 brooch by British artist Andrew Logan has a mirror fragment set in resin with coloured pastes and glitter trim.*

above right: *French Art Deco silver dress clips, c. 1920, set with white and coloured pastes to imitate the gem pieces of the period.*

above: *An unusual mixture of precious and imitation materials was used in this 1950s necklace and earring set by Schiaparelli, including coral and cultured pearl with paste, imitation pearl and base metal.*

In the early years of the twentieth century, costume jewellery largely copied the grand and vastly more expensive "originals" sported by the aristocracy and well-to-do, and costume jewels were thus worn exactly like their more costly counterparts. With the arrival of Art Deco, however, costume jewellery took on a life of its own, exploring new avenues of jewellery design.

The use of plastic in jewellery was not new. Many different types of plastic had been used in the nineteenth century, but purely to imitate other more costly materials such as ivory, tortoiseshell and amber rather than in their own right. Vulcanite, for example, was used as an alternative to jet following the increase in the demand for black mourning jewellery in Britain after the death of Queen Victoria's husband, Prince Albert, in 1861. New colour combinations found in the fashion and decor of the 1920s provided a new role for plastic as an imitation of jade, coral and onyx in the fabulous new Art Deco look. Along with strong new designs and colours came new ideas about when and how these innovative pieces could be worn. The strict regime of day and evening wear was broken and any jewel could be worn at any time and anywhere. Materials were used in their own right, as well as in loose interpretations of other more precious elements, and plastic and glass were quite acceptable and often combined in one glorious statement of fun.

With the world economic depression of the late 1920s, the light-hearted costume jewellery of the crazy Art Deco period began to disappear, and costume jewels were once again designed largely in imitation of "real" ones. Glamour became important in 1930s fashion, but the costs associated with such escapist desires were far greater than most women could even dream of meeting. So costume jewellery came to the rescue, and the wonderful creations of colourless paste from this decade enabled many women to feel just a little like the Hollywood film stars they envied and idolized. Bracelets and dress clips were everywhere, some set in silver but most in base white metals, echoing the popular style of screen goddesses such as Jean Harlow, the original platinum-blonde bombshell.

However, not all costume jewellery of the 1930s and 1940s imitated established mainstream jewellery styles. Some original designs flourished, and fun was still an essential ingredient. The seemingly way-out designs of the artist Salvador Dalí and dress designer Elsa Schiaparelli, for example, produced wonderful pea-pod

above: *A Joseff Hollywood necklace of "antique gold" coloured metal flowerheads with green paste centres, c. 1940.*

necklaces and themed pieces, such as a circus collection, which were too bizarre to be created from expensive metals and gems. Schiaparelli had started in the fashion business, and made fantastical decorative fastenings such as lobsters or acrobats for her clothes, design skills she then expanded into costume jewellery. She worked with many artists, including Dalí and Jean Schlumberger, through the 1930s and 1940s and her "junk jewellery", as she called it, became ever more bizarre and often quite witty, using a wide range of materials including plastics.

Hollywood not only inspired but also employed a number of jewellers including Eugene Joseff and William Hobe. Joseff's passion for jewellery and his interest in historical pieces helped him to establish himself as a creator of costume jewellery for the cinema. He made, reproduced and rented out pieces, especially for historical and epic films such as *Gone with the Wind* (1939) and *The Thief of Baghdad* (1940). These proved so popular that he started a retail line, which sold through many of the large stores in the United States, signed either "Joseff" or "Joseff of Hollywood". William Hobe was a member of the Hobe family who ran the eponymous jewellery firm established in Paris in the nineteenth century. Moving to the United States, he won a contract to produce costume jewellery for Florenz Ziegfeld, the producer of the famous revue show *The Ziegfeld Follies*. The fame of the Hobe company spread, and in the 1940s its advertisements used famous people in portraits taken by top photographers with the slogan

above: The fine work around the pastes makes this mid-twentieth century brooch immediately recognisable as a piece from the American firm Hobe.

"Jewels of Legendary Splendour". Often pieces were made from silver or gold-plated metal, using good glass or semi-precious stones in filigree work. Many of its jewels were also made for inclusion in films, and were worn by stars such as Joan Crawford. In 1943, William's sons Donald and Robert joined the firm, and they continue to run it and look after the important archive collection.

World War Two changed the direction of costume jewellery yet again. Much of the metal used in these fabulous imitations was now needed for munitions and the war effort, so manufacturers were forced to upgrade. During this period nearly all the pieces were made in silver, which was gilded to yield the rich gold colour so popular at the time. The vast majority of wartime costume jewellery was produced in the United States and these pieces are stamped "sterling", along with the maker's name. British pieces bear full silver hallmarks, and those from France bear a small *poinçon* (a small mark punched into the metal, usually an animal head or insect, that indicates the type and standard of the metal used). In Germany, a simple 800 stamp shows the standard of silver used, which was lower than the 925 silver of the American or British pieces. There was a rise in the demand for patriotic jewellery throughout the Allied nations, and this was quicker and easier to produce in costume jewellery, and was sometimes sold in aid of the war effort. These serious pieces were replaced towards the end of the war in 1945 by more light-hearted figural brooches. Expensive versions of these designs were also to be seen in the windows of the big jewellery houses soon after the war.

above: *These two American costume jewellery brooches are made of silver with paste decoration. The bullrush is by Pennino while the "clear belly" heron is by Trifari; both date from World War Two.*

Following the war, costume jewellery was once again manufactured from the non-precious metals used in the pre-war years, although the results were more refined and of better quality. New manufacturers and designs emerged, and the launch of Christian Dior's New Look (see page 77) included costume jewellery. These early Dior pieces were produced by Mitchel Maer and marked "Christian Dior by Mitchel Maer". From the mid-1950s they were made by Henkel and Grosse, and simply marked "Christian Dior" together with the year of manufacture. These jewels were typified by soft pastel colours and designs that reflected the return to feminine styles seen in the New Look, and have now become some of the most collected pieces of costume jewellery.

Many of the major designers of fashion jewellery and "luxury" jewellery went on to become important in the world of costume jewellery. One of these was Trifari, an American company whose designs heavily influenced costume jewellery during the post-war period. The designer Alfred Philippe had come to Trifari in 1930, having previously designed for Cartier and Van Cleef & Arpels, and produced many fine quality pieces for his new employer. These included costume jewels that were very like the invisibly set pieces made by Van Cleef & Arpels, except that Trifari versions appeared in non-precious metals or silver with plastic "clusters" of "gems". The company was soon to run into its own problems with imitators directly copying some of its designs, such as its trademark crown brooch, which had become immensely popular after Trifari became the first costume

left: *This Trifari carnation brooch was inspired by the invisibly set pieces produced by Van Cleef & Arpels. This example dates from the 1960s.*

jewellery company to advertise on a national scale, with the slogan "Jewels by Trifari", in 1938. The social acceptance and popularity of costume jewellery were confirmed in 1952 when Trifari won a legal action to copyright its designs. From then on all costume jewellery could bear the copyright symbol (a useful pointer for dating pieces). In 1956, Mrs Eisenhower, the wife of the President of the United States, ordered Trifari jewellery to wear at the presidential inaugural ball, thus giving costume jewellery the White House seal of approval. Alfred Philippe retired in 1968, following the production of his last collection entitled "Jewels of India", which fed the demand for ethnic designs at that time and proved a huge success.

The Italian firm of Coppola and Toppo started a new trend for elaborate designer pieces of costume jewellery. Established in the late 1940s, their exciting creations of strung glass beads in fabulous colours and combinations of exotic styles were produced in small numbers, and they designed a special collection for the American market. The fashion for crystal at the end of the 1950s raised the firm's popularity even further, and their jewellery commanded high prices in the collectors' market of the late 1980s.

Another highly collected designer is the American Kenneth Jay Lane. His work rose to prominence in the 1960s with his jewels being worn by Jackie Kennedy and later by other First Ladies such as Nancy Reagan and Barbara Bush. Indeed, Jacqueline Kennedy Onassis ordered one of the copies that he made of a necklace given to her by her new husband Aristotle Onassis, examples of which became an important part of any KJL collection. Inspired by many of the great jewellers, including Cartier and David Webb, Lane brought their style, along with his own, to people at an affordable price. This was continued when KJL jewels became available at under

$100 in many department stores, and they have even been sold through television shopping channels. Lane chooses his materials and construction methods carefully, designing the pieces himself; he has always preferred lasting classic designs to those aimed at satisfying short-term seasonal fashions. A superb collection of Lane's jewellery was handled by Christie's in New York in a single-owner sale at the beginning of the twenty-first century.

above: This style of necklace by Kenneth Jay Lane became immensely popular after being ordered by Jackie Onassis.

In the 1980s, the large white paste brooch made a comeback, and bold and brash "*Dallas*"-style paste jewellery was championed and popularized by, among others, Butler and Wilson of London. The styles of the 1990s were more discreet and costume jewellery was in plentiful supply, with many specialist accessory shops appearing in most major shopping areas in both Europe and the United States. This explosion of decorative-jewellery outlets furnished the passer-by with up-to-the-minute fashion colours and shapes at low prices.

THE DI PORTANOVA JEWELS

The Baron and Baroness di Portanova were sophisticated members of the international jet set with houses in Houston and Acapulco where they entertained the rich and famous. The houses were crammed full of magnificent pictures, furniture and objets de vertu. Recalling a dinner party at River Oaks, Houston, one guest wrote: "Forty people were beside the pool at tables that Sandra, The Baroness, had caused to be set with their Salvador Dalí vermeil flatware together with the huge "Moth and flame" candelabras, which illuminated the event." Works of art by Fragonard and Canaletto were combined with fine furniture purchased from the Rothschild collection, Egyptian and Estruscan antiquities and oriental treasures to create luxurious settings suitable for their lifestyle.

The estate sale of their collection of jewels in October 2000 gave a fascinating insight into the jewel case required for the jet-set lifestyle in the late twentieth century, with an index of makers that spanned the world. The sale opened with a surrealist gold pendant to a design by Salvador Dalí, modelled as a combination spoon, comb and watch face, and was followed by a beaten gold torc (ancient neck ring) necklace typical of the work of Ilias Lalaounis of Greece. Among an abundance of Bulgari daytime jewellery in the collection

❶

were a series of gold close-curb-link neck chains in combinations of white and yellow gold with diamond detail – including a suite of belt, necklace and bracelet set with antique British silver coins – together with other necklaces incorporating antiquities. These included a fifth-century BC agate scarab, the base carved with a pictorial *intaglio* of a gryphon, a fifteenth-century bronze medallion inscribed Sigismondo Pandolfo Malatesta and a British George III gold guinea. In each case the reverse of the mount was neatly engraved with details of the inset "*objets*", making the piece both a decoration and a subject of discussion.

Rings and earrings, all mounted in yellow gold with cabochon-cut brightly coloured rubies, sapphires and emeralds within a field of pavé-set diamonds and enhanced in some cases by enamel, were matched by a cultured-pearl choker necklace with gem-set panels signed "Marina B". This was the signature of Marina Bulgari, the granddaughter of Sotiro Bulgari, the founder of Bulgari. Marina learnt her craft in the workshop of her father Constantino with such success that in 1979 she opened the first Marina B boutique in Rome to glowing reviews. Her collection combines extravagant gems, many cut in her own distinctive modified heart shape, with exquisitely made gold in modern innovative colour combinations. Marina B boutiques are now situated in Geneva, London, Milan, New York, Jeddah and Riyadh ensuring the international flavour of this popular style.

When accompanying the baroness as she set forth in her sea-green Rolls-Royce in ball gown and jewels, Ricky, the baron, could choose from an extensive collection of cufflinks in gold, diamond and enamel by Cartier, Asprey and the Italian firm Massoni, previously jewellers to the Italian royal family. On his wrist would be a fine watch, possibly his Cartier Tank model enhanced with diamonds and matching the more delicate version owned by his wife. For use at less formal gatherings, the baroness had a collection of amusing cocktail jewellery. This included bright red coral oval cabochons in diamond lion frames, a pair of enamel tiger-head ear clips with gaping red mouths and diamond whiskers, and a textured eighteen-carat white and yellow gold Fu dog brooch with diamond mane, paws and tail, cabochon chrysoprase eyes and drop-cut ruby tongue, as well as a charming suite of diamond and green enamel frog jewellery with sapphire eyes. Indian faceted ruby, emerald and sapphire beads were combined with baroque cultured pearls to create a colourful chandelier-drop suite of necklace, earrings and pendant.

The tiger economies of Asia have given rise to some innovative designers including Kai-Yin Lo, who devoted her design skills to jewellery in 1979 and created a bold and

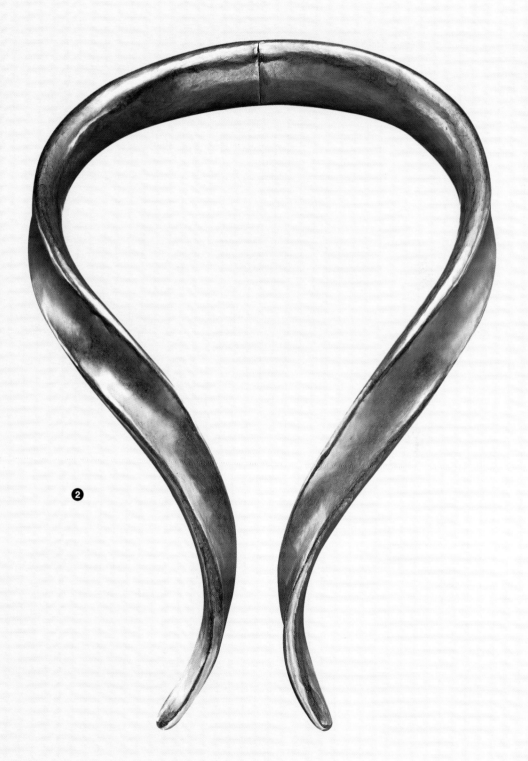

1 A marquise and rectangular-cut diamond-set choker necklace by Marina B.
2 This hinged scrolling gold collar necklace is by Ilias Lalaounis.

❸

amusing cabochon gem and silver-gilt starfish brooch for the baroness. Colourful gems including tourmaline, peridot and turquoise, carved, shaped and polished to fit the design, appeared in dramatic butterfly and flower brooches made by Boucheron and Bulgari in the 1980s. Accessories were important. Evening bags featured in both white and yellow gold were treated as brocade or basket weave set with diamonds, and there was a wardrobe of watches in rectangular tank, coiled flexible gas pipe "Tubogas" and machine-inspired screw-head detail by Cartier, Bulgari and Harry Winston.

Carved rock crystal became a feature of Italian jewellery in the late twentieth century and appeared often in the di Portanova collection – as a shaped frame for a heart-shaped

diamond necklace and earrings, for example, or the body of a carved elephant pendant, both by Bulgari. The collection also contained an impressive range of rock crystal, gem and gold table sculptures by Boucheron, including a charming rock-crystal cat relaxing on an amethyst cushion with white and yellow gold tassel corners. Other sculptures were carved as eagles, parrots, cranes, frogs and snails, the rock crystal sparkling in the light yet blending well with the carved marble fittings in the di Portanova homes.

As a trendsetter it was important that the baroness should recognize and adopt forthcoming fashions, so in the early 1980s she was among the first to acquire a single strand of fine Australian South Sea cultured pearls ranging in size from 12.27 to 15.6 millimetres (about half an inch to five-eighths of an inch) with a diamond ball clasp, to be worn with any of the diamond and cultured-pearl earrings set in gold for daytime, and white gold for evening. Impressive jewellery by David Webb (1925–75), the prolific designer who worked with Nina Silberstein and whose New York store continues to realize his designs under the direction of the Silberstein family, included a grand cabochon sapphire, diamond and turquoise suite, the bold colours dominating the gold and platinum mounts. Among the collection of earrings were two important pairs from the Bulgari family. The first,

3 A pair of diamond drop earrings by Marina B, composed of graduated tassels of rose-cut diamonds.

4 A pair of less formal earrings by Marina B, set with diamonds, emeralds, rubies and onyx.

5 A colourful bracelet by Massoni, set with rubies, sapphires, emeralds and diamonds.

by Marina B, comprised a cascade of graduated rose-cut diamond lines in simple spectacle-frame mounts from pavé diamond tops; the second, for formal occasions, was a pair of striking pendant earrings that incorporated emeralds, baguette diamonds and a pair of yellow diamonds each weighing nearly ten carats. These diamonds were accompanied by Gemological Institute of America certificates, which described both of them as natural fancy intense yellow colour, 9.85 and 9.70 carats and VVS2 and VS1 clarity, the second stone with a working diagram indicating how the clarity could be improved by the removal of surface faults.

Coloured diamonds also featured in jewellery by Marchak of Paris and Massoni of Rome, combining shades of brown, yellow and near colourless to create autumnal hues. Massoni was the creator of some of the most flamboyant gems in the collection: a suite of carved ruby, sapphire, emerald and diamond floral necklace, bracelet and earrings, recalling the 1930s tutti-frutti jewellery of Cartier. A monkey and banana suite in gold, pavé-set with diamonds and gems, the polished gold bands of bananas with carved emerald leaves sought by climbing and stretching monkeys, reflected the cartoon humour of Walt Disney. The need for traditional fine jewellery for grand balls was filled by a flexible diamond collar-necklace set with numerous drop-cut, marquise and brilliant-cut diamonds with matching bracelet and earrings, the earrings terminating in a pair of drop-cut diamonds weighing sixteen carats each. Reflecting the durability and current popularity of Art Deco jewellery, the collection also included a pair of Art Deco diamond clip-brooches designed as a baguette diamond and pavé-set diamond interlacing ribbon, enhanced with twin rows of graduated brilliant-cut diamonds mounted in platinum. There was also an Art Deco diamond bracelet from the mid-1930s, set with three large rectangular-cut diamonds and numerous baguette-cut diamonds mounted in platinum.

The entire collection demonstrates the eclectic nature of late twentieth-century jewellery fashion, combining as it does whimsy, sentimentality and exhibitionism with inspiration deriving from many cultures and periods. The one defining feature is a deep appreciation of fine workmanship, still easily obtained by the rich and famous, as it was at the beginning of the century. Yet this collection also included recent fine work in more minor pieces – quality has spread to fill a wider price range.

chapter six

THE MODERN MARKET

TRENDS AND MARKETING

The average jeweller, whether an independent shop, part of a family-run group, a large retail chain or in a department store, has generally shown some resistance to major change. Sticking to the tried and tested big four – diamond, sapphire, ruby and emerald – they are nervous when faced with alternatives, and generally tend to cater to any changes in fashion and trend at the lower end of the market. However, the public are now beginning to demand a greater variety of jewels, and improved standards and services.

Jewellery design must now adapt to the lifestyle of the consumer, and yet also offer some continuity with the past and tradition by continuing to offer certain classic pieces such as the diamond ring. For this is still considered the ultimate decoration and status symbol, and the solitaire remains the most popular style. However, even the solitaire must adapt. Although a setting raised high off the finger has been popular in the United States for some time, many now prefer a simple platinum claw (vertical projecting prongs) or white gold rub-over setting (bent over the girdle of the gem) with a band kept low for practicality in today's active world.

Consumers are also increasingly asking for certification of the stones they buy. The demand for certified diamonds, those with a proven colour and clarity, increased tremendously within the last decade of the twentieth century and, although jewellers have been slow to react, we are now seeing more certificates offered as part of a standard selling procedure. Gold is still popular, and more and more customers are now demanding that articles sold as gold contain a majority of that metal, and not the nine parts in twenty-four of British nine-carat gold in which the balance is largely made up of copper. (Eighteen-carat gold, in contrast, is seventy-five per cent gold.)

Chains, bangles, bracelets, earrings and necklaces in easy-to-wear styles are useful adjuncts to daytime jeans and T-shirts, but the jeweller must now also carry body-piercing jewellery, such as nose studs, body bars and body rings. There is also a demand for ear-cuffs for the top of the ear, toe rings, thumb rings (popular in Europe three or four hundred years ago and briefly reintroduced in the hippy styles of the 1960s) and jewelled false nails.

At the lower end of the market, the quartz family of gems – amethyst, citrine and rose quartz – has increased in popularity. Set in silver and sometimes combined with garnet, they create a simple, yet modern, look. The mid-price pieces may include various shades of tourmaline, peridot, aquamarine, blue topaz and tanzanite. As more publicity is given to the wide range of enhancements to which emerald, ruby and sapphire are subjected (see pages 92–5), there is a growing enthusiasm for gems that

left: *Three of the most popular styles of traditional diamond rings, the ever-popular single stone, the reliable three-stone and the more recently re-appreciated rectangular cut.*

are untreated and natural, such as the reds and greens of tourmaline and African garnet, which can appear in any colour except blue.

"Power bracelets" made up of beads of various stones were promoted through the 1990s and are the latest manifestation of an ancient belief in the ability of gems to aid the body and mind with their inherent powers. Some are advertised as Buddhist inspired and described as radiating energy and bringing peace and harmony. Different stones are believed to have different powers. Amethyst promotes intuition and intelligence (the Romans believed it could protect against drunkenness); garnet fosters creativity; clear quartz brings inner peace and wisdom; haematite offers stability and peace; and rose quartz opens the heart to love and heals past hurt. It is a measure of the appeal of gems that such claims can stand up without proof in our scientific world and be accepted and put into practice, even if only on the basis that they do no harm.

The pearl has now been entirely replaced in popular jewellery by the cultured pearl, which is produced in enormous quantities, particularly in China, but is still an important ingredient in both traditional and modern designs. An alternative to the round pearl is the mabé cultured pearl, a hemispherical blister cultivated on the inner shell of the oyster, which is then cut from the shell, filled with wax and backed by mother-of-pearl to produce an economical half-pearl of good size. Some are left with their mother-of-pearl surround which, when cut to shape, can be incorporated into the design of a jewel.

The flood of amber from the Dominican Republic was the result of increased demand caused by the high-profile and immensely popular *Jurassic Park* films of the 1990s. This has now slowed to a more gentle trickle as the fantasy of dinosaurs' D.N.A. carried by mosquitoes frozen in

left: *A piece of day-wear jewellery by Bulgari, this long chain is excellent for dressing up casual clothes.*

time has become stale. The thirty-million-year-old fossilized tree sap materialized in mounds of beads and silver-mounted pendants, rings and earrings in mainstream popular jewellery, whereas it had previously mainly been used in so-called "ethnic" jewellery. Now jewellers' windows that were recently dominated by the yellows and browns of

top: The popularity of tourmaline has increased with the interest in new colours and materials; this bracelet contains various shades and colours.

above: A mabé cultured pearl and haematite pendant necklace.

amber are home to the wonderful range of colour offered by the tourmaline, quartz and garnet groups of gems cut in new styles that emphasize colour and reflection.

Popular fancy cuts include the "buff top", which incorporates a smooth domed top over a faceted base, and the "chequer board" with square facets on its domed tops. Alongside traditional methods of cutting and polishing gems, new methods of shaping with lasers, controlled by computer programs, produce complex and intriguing stones that can be reproduced exactly time and time again, facilitating the use of standard cast settings. Many jewellers have developed a house style, a recognizable range of goldwork and gems that may be named and promoted, in much the same way as a fashion house promotes its latest season's clothes.

In the mid- to top-range market, as finance to support high-quality services becomes concentrated in a few groups, many of the big names in jewellery have joined forces with the suppliers of other luxury goods and services to offer luxury lifestyle packages. Bulgari, famous for its jewellery, watches and leather goods, has recently set up a joint venture with the hotel group Marriott International to enter the luxury hotel market as Bulgari Hotels and Resorts. The hotels will be designed by the company to reflect the best in Italian design and cuisine and make Bulgari the ultimate luxury brand statement. Similarly, the Italian fashion house Versace has already opened a luxury hotel on Australia's Gold Coast, and the auctioneers Christie's has been purchased by a French entrepreneur to become part of a massive luxury-market empire. LVMH is the largest luxury goods group and includes Moët, Hennessy, Louis Vuitton, Chaumet, Christian Dior, Fred, Fendi and the watch brands Zenith, Ebel, and Tag Heuer. They now also have an arrangement with De Beers to open stores selling De Beers branded diamond jewellery. Pinault Printemps Redoute (PPR) has expanded into the luxury goods market with the purchase of Christie's, and it has a major interest in the Gucci group, which includes Yves Saint

Laurent and Boucheron. Richemont, a Swiss-based group that covers fashion, retail and gun-making, includes Cartier, Van Cleef & Arpels, Piaget, International Watch Co., Lange & Sohne, Jaeger-LeCoultre, Vacheron and Constantin, Baume and Mercier, Montblanc and Alfred Dunhill. The Swatch group has steadily absorbed the Swiss watch market and now embodies Omega, Rado, Mido, Flik Flak, Pierre Balmain, Longines, Tissot, Hamilton, Certina, Blancpain, Calvin Klein, Breguet, Glashutte, Leon Hatot and Jacquet-Droz.

Supporting bodies, such as the World Gold Council, strive to promote the use of gold in jewellery through international competitions and corporate advertising, with particular emphasis on the most active markets for using and buying gold including India, Turkey, the Gulf States, Mexico and Vietnam. There are also more special-ized trade organizations like that for the Tahitian pearl industry, Perles de Tahiti, which conducts a worldwide Tahitian pearl jewellery competition. This has various categories for ladies' and gentlemen's jewellery with the provision that Tahitian pearls must account for at least fifty per cent of the total value of precious materials employed. Another similar competition for diamond-jew-ellery design is run by De Beers, the De Beers Diamond International Awards (see pages 89 and 121).

The media in all its forms is, of course, a vital tool for promoting jewellery to the public. Events such as the Academy Award ceremonies for the film industry held annually in the United States see actresses and celebrities

such as Kate Hudson, Jennifer Lopez, Sigourney Weaver and Julie Andrews glitter-ing in diamonds borrowed from Harry Winston and Fred Leighton. Julia Roberts has favoured Van Cleef & Arpels, Penelope Cruz has worn diamonds from Bulgari and Catherine Zeta Jones sported a fifty-carat aquamarine necklace lent by H. Stern. Harry Winston's diamonds have also decorated Faye Dunaway, and Michelle Yeoh once wore a dress studded with 180,000 Swarovski crystals. As people adore watching celebrities and love to know who made their dresses and jewellery, these events are a perfect opportunity for jewellers to advertise their wares and get their names linked to the famous. Indeed, such exposure can influence the sales of specific pieces of jewellery and start new trends.

All designers benefit from a well-publicized commission, so London designer Stephen Webster was delighted to be asked to supply the wedding rings for the marriage of singer Madonna and film director Guy Ritchie in 2000, his jewellery having been a favourite of Madonna for several years. The bride's broad brushed-platinum band was studded with diamonds, while the groom's more traditional platinum band featured en-graved scrollwork. Webster's 2001 "Rose and Crown" collection was based on the "hot" colours of recently introduced gems, including pink tourmaline and vivid orange mandarin garnet.

above: *This ring is made from one complete piece of peridot that has a polished top and circular cut peridots in an applied white gold mount, by Catherine Prevost.*

below: *A speciman of amber showing the trapped flying ants inside.*

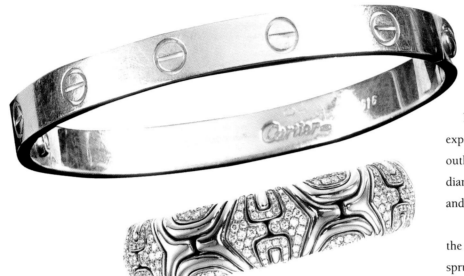

traditional coloured gems to create striking modern pieces with the appeal of the unusual. In four years the company sold some 3,500 pieces of significant jewellery set with black diamonds, and it has now firmly established its position in the luxury jewellery market. From its Geneva base it has expanded to London, Rome and Gstaad, and has franchise outlets in Moscow, Paris and the United States. The black diamond range now includes luxury watches, sunglasses and mobile-phone covers, and continues to expand.

Black mounts have also become fashionable. Carnet, the company owned by designer Michelle Ong, has sprung to prominence with individual creations drawn from nature, Asian culture and antique lace, which use high-quality gems in surprising colour combinations, often with black oxidized-gold mounts. Her jewels also incorporate innovative gem forms such as cut sections of drusy mineral specimens, a bed of tiny sparkling crystals which have formed naturally on a rock base, such as amethyst on agate or the brilliant green but tiny uvarovite garnet on black chromite.

Yellow gold is beginning to make a comeback after a decade of white gold dominance, but platinum is still viewed as the ultimate luxury metal and is increasingly popular in Japan and China. Big and bold necklaces in silver, gold and platinum match casual open-neck fashions, and allow a wide range of surface treatments. The trend towards large areas of worked metal has particular appeal to designers such as the Americans David Yurman and Michael Good. Both men began their careers as sculptors. David Yurman was an apprentice to the Cubist master Jacques Lipschitz before turning to the art of jewellery design. His signature metal-cable jewellery is crafted to move with and relate to the curves of the human body

Hollywood glamour has never lost its appeal and the jewellery bought and worn by the stars is a major influence. Loree Rodkin gave up her position as manager of some of Hollywood's hottest actors to design and create jewellery, which is purchased by some of her former clients, including Brad Pitt, Sarah Jessica Parker and Robert Downey, Jr. Her design collection is now distributed across the United States, including Neiman Marcus stores, and in Europe and Asia.

While Harry Winston is well established and known for fabulous diamonds in simple platinum settings, newcomers must establish their own market niche, a requirement well understood by the Swiss company de Grisogono which launched its black diamond jewellery collection in 1997. Previously black diamonds have, in the main, been dismissed as industrial material, except for the larger stones, but here was a daring range of jewellery that used black and white diamonds in combination with

top: *An eighteen-carat gold Cartier "love bangle", designed as a series of screw-heads; the clasp is a screw device which needs the accompanying screwdriver to open.*

above: *First seen in 1988, this gold and diamond bracelet by Bulgari is of the "Alveare" design.*

above: *A diamond and black diamond*
necklace by Carnet.

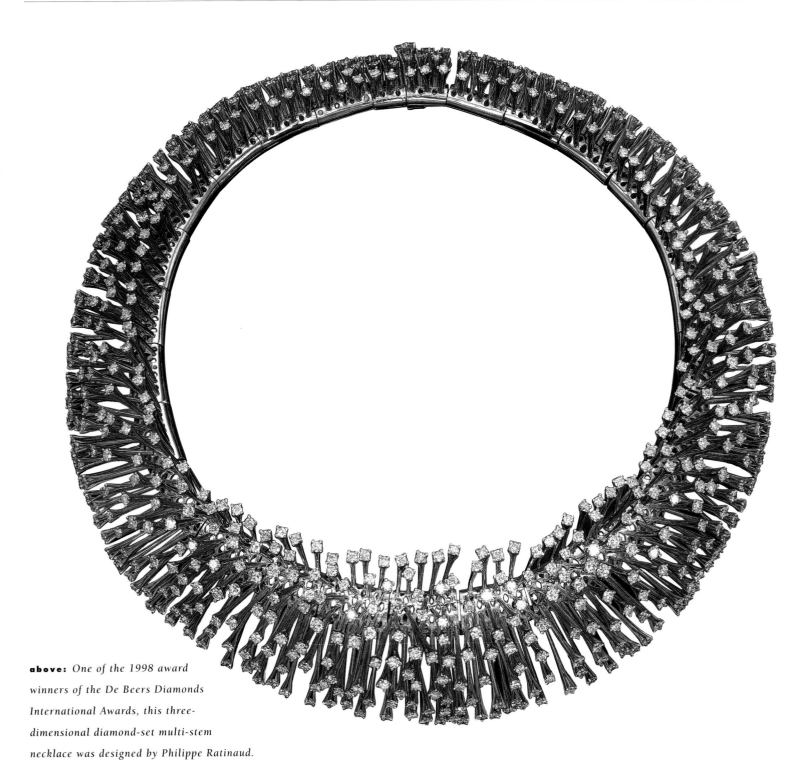

above: *One of the 1998 award winners of the De Beers Diamonds International Awards, this three-dimensional diamond-set multi-stem necklace was designed by Philippe Ratinaud.*

and evolves year by year into new forms. Michael Good, a self-taught sculptor and jeweller, specializes in a form of metalworking called "anti-clastic raising" in which the edges of a sheet of metal are compressed while the centre is stretched, resulting in a distinctive double curvature at a ninety-degree angle. Although innovative, he continues to be very aware that, unlike sculpture, jewellery needs to be wearable and in harmony with the client's taste.

The fashion for logos, although not as intense as in the 1980s, is still in evidence. Versace capitalized on this with its "Diffusion" collection based on a gold letter "V". This is cleverly used as a slide on a "lariat"-style neck chain, similar to the traditional necktie worn by American cowboys, and the motif appears on all the accessories in its range of leather ware, clothes and perfumes, thus uniting the luxury brand.

As one door closes another opens, and the recent bad publicity for emeralds, which revealed that many stones are treated without this being disclosed, has led to an increase in the demand for alternative green gems.

Tsavorite (a bright green garnet), green tourmaline and peridot have all enjoyed a recent surge in popularity, which coincided with a far greater use of all shades of green in the fashion world at the end of the twentieth century. The green stones team well with yellow gold, and David Yurman has used this combination in his limited-edition couture pieces and incorporated some of his own collection of rare peridots of fifty to sixty carats each.

above: The textured cable design of this suite of gold jewellery by David Webb gives evidence to the popularity of strong gold jewellery with casual clothes.

The location of the retail outlet is of course of great importance and for the top design houses it has to be of the calibre of Place Vendôme in Paris, Bond Street in London or Madison Avenue in New York. In New York, Bulgari, Chopard, Cartier, Laurence Graff, Chatila and David Yurman can all be found among the top fashion boutiques between 57th and 72nd Streets. The area has a more intimate feel than Fifth Avenue with its big outlets, and is preferred by wealthy discriminating buyers looking for unique designs. Aaran Basha, well known for his "baby shoes" and "ladybug" whimsical jewels, opened his Madison Avenue boutique in 1990, a time when Depression and failing businesses created opportunities to acquire premises that would otherwise be unobtainable. Basha is willing to explore gaps in the market and combines his innovative designs with briolette-cut diamonds (a reintroduced traditional Indian multi-faceted cutting of drop-shaped diamonds) or with the new coloured diamonds, including pinks and yellows. As the reputation of Madison Avenue has grown, its select client base has expanded and now embraces customers from Europe, Saudi Arabia, Kuwait and South America as well as the whole of North America.

In Southeast Asia, the so-called "tiger" economies have suffered great setbacks since the late 1990s. However, the jewellery industries of China, Taiwan, Thailand and Indonesia are poised for new growth, and looking to secure markets in the United States, South America and Europe. To this end, many Asian designers and South Sea pearl traders exhibit at the Basel International Trade Fair to establish worldwide contacts.

India is a vast market, and one that has started to open up since the ending of their Gold Control Act in 1992. Previously serviced by traditional local jewellers, the Indian market is now experiencing the full force of western design and marketing, with Cartier and Tiffany both opening retail outlets. Swarovski of Austria,

right: *A late 1990s necklace of emerald and diamond beads suspending a briolette-cut yellow diamond drop.*

producers of crystal ornaments, faux gems and jewellery, has established a manufacturing plant to create and produce new designs and products for this market. The duty-free zone in Bombay allows Indian manufacturers to compete on the international market without the handicap of additional national tax and duty. The new market forces are a major change for the Indian population, which previously viewed gold jewellery – often in the form of a dowry – as an investment and a hedge against inflation. Jewellery as a fashion statement and status symbol is an emerging concept for the middle classes who are now susceptible to advertising promoting branded goods. De Beers and the Platinum Guild International hope to see increases in expenditure in their markets in the region of twenty to thirty per cent a year. While many of the Indian companies involved in this expansion are new to the market, there is a pool of experience to draw upon. Shrenuj and Co. Ltd, for example, was established in 1906 to export polished diamonds and became one of the select band of Diamond Trading Co. sightholders, who could purchase parcels of rough diamond crystals direct from De Beers, in 1983. They export to Europe and the United States. Responding to market requirements, they became an authorized platinum manufacturer and distributor for the Platinum Guild International in 1990.

To counter the bad press covering the enhancement of gems and the infiltration of synthetic ones, gem marketing groups are coming together to promote their

above: *This diamond and grey Tahitian cultured pearl and multi-gem "Jaipur" necklace by Mauboussin incorporates peridot, amethyst and pink tourmaline to provide an Indian flavour.*

combined products. For example, the Minas Gems Consortium represents seven Brazilian wholesalers who together certify their gem production for authenticity and quality, and ensure fair pricing. They are supported by Brazil's Export Agency and participate in the trade fairs, provide information and training and lobby for better trade laws. Internationalization and co-operation has been generally enhanced by the development of the Internet, which allows all strata of the industry access to an enormous market. Even the independent opal mines of Australia, which are still worked with a pick and bucket, have banded together to launch an online trading platform for the sale of rough and cut opals, and to broadcast news of recent finds and developments on their site. Yet, there are still mixed feelings regarding the Internet as a marketing tool for luxury goods. Most of the top houses use their sites for information and promotional material to encourage consumers to visit their stores where the traditional service standards can be maintained. However, there is a growing demand for high-value branded goods to be available instantly, and there is little doubt that the new generation of computer-comfortable business people will expect to be able to shop from their desk or home for almost all occasions, using the certificated information now available to purchase the stone or stones that they require. This is, of course, part of the reasoning behind the luxury trade conglomerates, who hope to be able to service important clients with all they need to maintain their affluent lifestyle. Although this does depend on the education of the purchaser to enable them to buy with confidence.

AVOIDING PROBLEMS

The jewellery trade is founded on trust, and at all the international diamond bourses (market buildings specific to diamond dealers) major financial deals are sealed with a handshake, and valuable goods change hands throughout the trade on verbal agreement. Such trust also leads to an almost secret society where little is said to the outside world about the inner workings of the business. However, with current advances in the technology of altering and reproducing natural products, and well-publicized cases of litigation over poorly described gems, good jewellers have had to become far more communicative with their clients. The customers are protected by many different laws and regulations, like the Trades Description Act in Britain, and by regulatory bodies such as CIBJO, which translates as the International Confederation of Jewellery, Silverware, Diamonds, Pearls and Stones. The oldest consumer-protection system in existence is the British hallmarking system, founded in the fourteenth century and still guaranteeing the quality of gold, silver and platinum today. Although this is now under review as it does not cater for the free interplay of goods across the European market, and cannot be adapted to modern market trends where metals are mixed. Thus the creative designs of Antonio Piluso, marketed as the Piligio brand, with their combinations of varicoloured and oxidized gold with iron, fail the

left: *This Rolex Oyster Perpetual Datejust wristwatch is manufactured using stainless steel and gold, presenting a problem for the British hallmarking system.*

far left: *Examining gems and jewellery closely can reveal information not readily visible to the naked eye, such as natural or synthetic origins, treatments and repairs.*

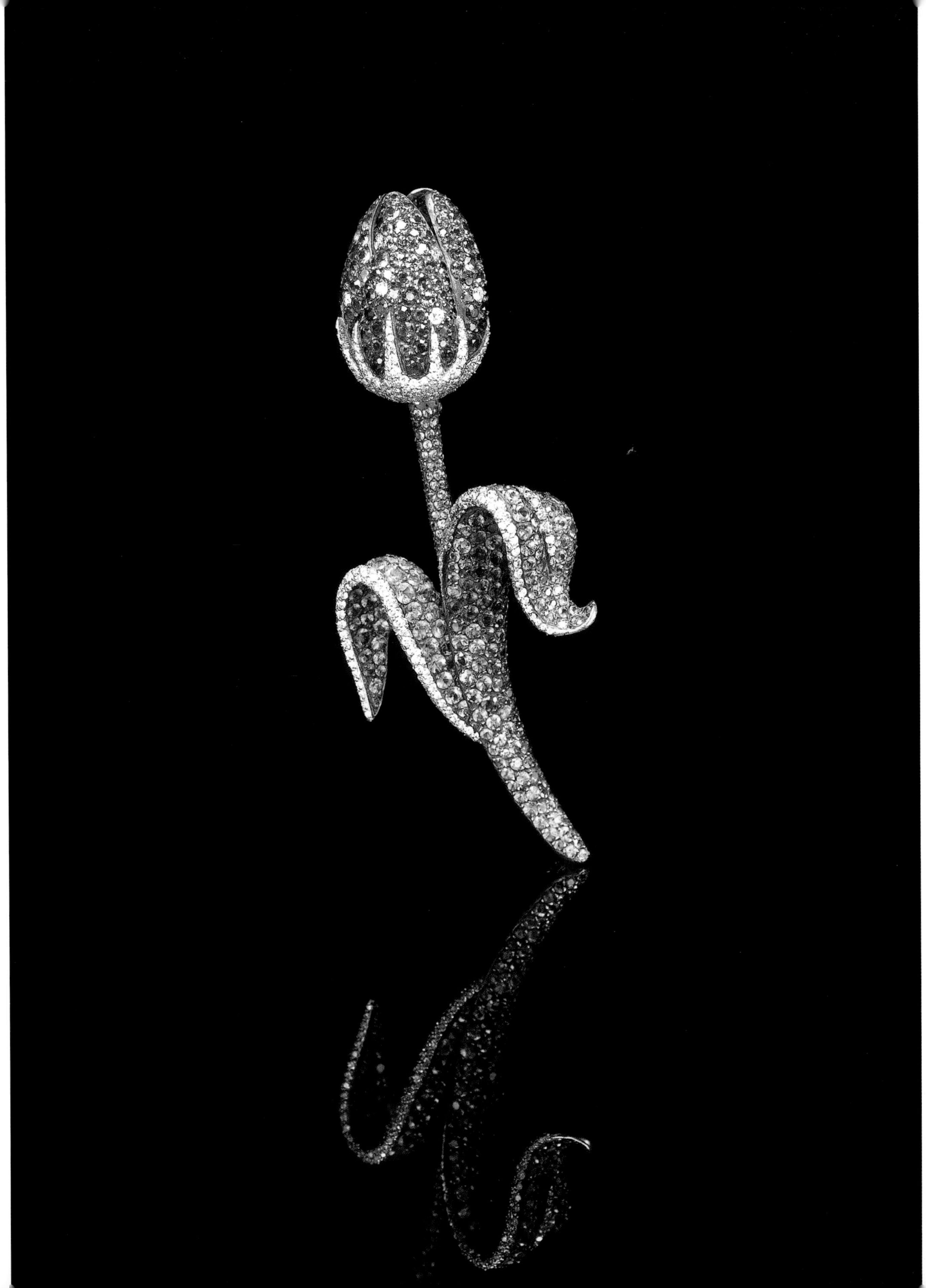

far left: *A fine example of new colour combinations, this tulip brooch is set with amethyst and pink sapphires, with diamond detail and tsavorite garnet stem and leaves.*

below: *These diamond and coloured stone band rings from the late 1990's currently depend on the jeweller for a description of the stones, but a similar grading system to that of diamonds may be introduced for coloured stones such as rubies, emeralds and sapphires.*

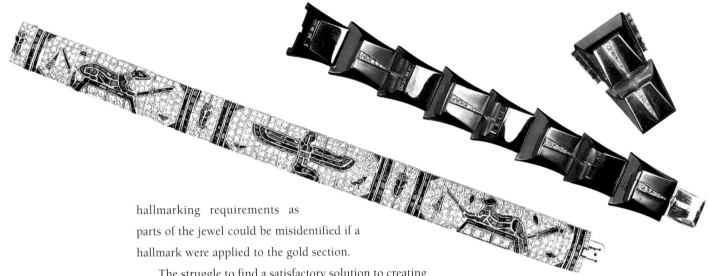

hallmarking requirements as parts of the jewel could be misidentified if a hallmark were applied to the gold section.

The struggle to find a satisfactory solution to creating unrestricted fair trade is also faced by the diamond trade, parts of which have been accused of funding wars in Africa by buying stones from rebel-run mines. Buyers are now asking where their diamonds originate, and this is leading to a complete redesign of the diamond buying and sorting structure so that stones can be guaranteed to be

left: This is a modern version of the popular Egyptian-motif bracelet fashionable in the Art Deco period.

right: A strong retro design normally attributed to the 1940s is seen in this diamond, ruby and gold bracelet and clip set, but it was actually made and hallmarked in Birmingham in 1962.

"conflict free". The certificate that accompanies a diamond not only details its quality in an approved and comparable terminology, but also guarantees the "morality" of the stone's extraction and is sometimes accompanied by a symbol laser-etched on to the girdle of the diamond. Such certificates also state that the gem has not been subjected to heat or pressure treatment to improve colour or clarity and, of course, certify that the diamond is a product of nature and not the laboratory. Similarly, although some treatment is traditionally accepted for coloured stones, it is important that the degree to which the gem has been enhanced is qualified and information on the long-term stability of such enhancements is made available. Today's retailer must be well informed about the product, not only with regard to fashion but also to the background of the jewels, the source of the gems, their degree of enhancement, long-term stability and the methods of guaranteeing all these factors.

The power of public opinion has been demonstrated by the legal restrictions on, and general aversion towards, products such as tortoiseshell and ivory. These materials are now only morally acceptable in antique pieces produced long before the species were threatened with extinction, and it is important that all natural organic materials used, be they coral, mother-of-pearl or ebony, are obtained from sustainable and managed environments.

Establishing trading standards that are meaningful worldwide becomes even more important with the growth of electronic marketing. Purchasing items unseen lends itself more to established branded goods than to fashion and design items, but is used successfully by diamond traders selling certified stones. Such activity means that the terminology must be internationally agreed, as are the grading standards of the Gemological Institute of America. This will lead in due course to international agreement on colour definition for coloured gems, and a certificate similar to that issued on diamonds will soon be provided for the currently uncategorized coloured stones.

Problems in jewellery do not only concern the raw materials, but also arise in connection with the finished articles. As certain styles or pieces by particular makers increase in value, so does the possibility that they will be reproduced, either as a fake deliberately manufactured to deceive or just as a "tribute" to that particular style. The revival in popularity of a design style from the past often results in new pieces being made in that style. At various times during the twentieth century, the urge to look back for inspiration became so strong that the resultant pieces of jewellery exactly resemble those from a totally different era, or even a different century.

The Edwardians had a passion for all things eighteenth-century, from jewellery through to furniture. So some pieces that may look like early paste may well have been manufactured in 1907 rather than 1709. The trained eye will see that the cut of the paste is usually wrong – it will probably resemble the Victorian brilliant cut, which had not been devised in the eighteenth-century. The settings may also differ subtly, but it is not always easy to tell without a comparison piece.

Design in the 1950s took a brief journey back to the nineteenth century and emulated Victorian looks. Black onyx with small pearls and textured surrounds and tassels

may look authentic, but the fittings will betray their more modern manufacture, and the pieces will have original safety catches rather than the replacement catches usually found on nineteenth-century pieces. This confusion between "revival" pieces and originals seems to be even more common in costume jewellery.

One of the strong inspirations behind 1960s design was Art Deco. There are now hundreds of pieces from this decade that are often mistaken for 1920s and 1930s originals. Now that the 1960s pieces are themselves forty or so years old, and marked with the patina of age, dating can be tricky. It can sometimes take a

below: *A paste set costume jewellery clip by "Eisenberg Original". This one is a 1930s original and not a recent copy.*

specialist in Art Deco to distinguish the original from the later piece, especially as the same materials and types of fitting were quite often used.

The 1970s and 1980s revival of the Arts and Crafts and Art Nouveau styles also leads to some confusion, although the quality of the later pieces tends to be inferior and much of it was machine-made. In addition, some of the later revival pieces have British hallmarks, so the date of manufacture can be easily ascertained.

As soon as something becomes so popular that it commands a premium, someone somewhere will try to fake it. During the surge of interest in costume jewellery shown in the 1980s, collectors fought for examples by the Eisenberg company, the most popular being those marked Eisenberg Original. These were changing hands in America for hundreds, sometimes thousands, of dollars, and it was only a matter of time before modern copies

were produced. As the original 1930s pieces were designed as loose imitations of diamond jewellery, the 1980s pieces were fakes of fakes!

The higher the quality of the piece being copied, the better the forgery must be to stand a chance of being convincing, and this is often an aid to identification. Some so-called "Cartier" pieces are sometimes genuinely from the period with a later faked signature, or they may be straightforward complete copies. It has been known for Cartier to confiscate and destroy fakes of its watches and jewels, and photographs of steamrollers poised to destroy hundreds of watches covering the road ahead have been published by the company as a warning.

There has always been a problem with base metals being disguised as gold, silver or platinum, alongside various imitations of diamonds and gems. Identifying man-made gems is becoming increasingly difficult as most new synthetics are so hard to separate from the natural stones that many can only be distinguished by laboratory tests, while some natural examples can now be so heavily treated and altered that they are often no longer acceptable as natural gems.

Finally, when does extensive repair work become a rebuild? Sometimes, so little of the original material remains in a piece that the jewellery borders on losing its genuine quality. All repairs will affect the value of a jewel in proportion to the extent of the work done. The poorer the repairs, either in number or quality (large amounts of badly applied lead-solder, for instance), the lower the value. When other pieces are introduced this is usually seen not as an honest repair but as a marriage of various

left: *A gentleman's gold and diamond-set "Diabolo" wristwatch by Cartier.*

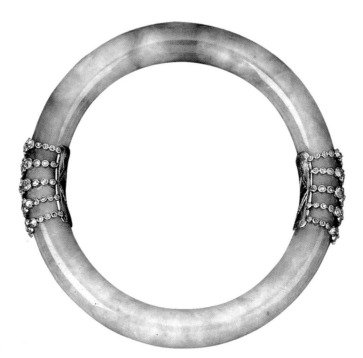

components. It can be misleading if the jewel is represented not as a decorative piece of jewellery but as an original and complete design of a certain era.

It is essential to buy jewellery from a respected member of the jewellery trade, and ideally the jeweller or dealer should be a member of a recognized professional body held in good esteem by the country in which they operate. Buying jewellery as an investment should not be a short-term consideration as, like buying a new car, a piece bought retail will lose a large percentage of its value (representing the store's profit, tax and a proportion of the manufacturing and design costs) as it is carried from the shop. Buy for the pleasure of giving or wearing, and if you have bought wisely you should have acquired a good hedge against inflation as well as an attractive piece of jewellery.

above: *An attractive jade and diamond bangle with diamond-set mounts made to hide the fact that the bangle is broken.*

THE REBIRTH OF THE GEMSTONE

Most of the dramatic changes to jewellery in the twentieth century came about because of huge alterations in society, be it war, economic depression, exciting inventions, new methods of travel or the changing role of women. Yet in the 1960s an alteration to gem cutting, which was so great that it would affect jewellery forever, was instigated by just one man – Bernd Munsteiner.

In an area of Germany known for stone cutting for over five hundred years, the Munsteiner family has had several generations active in this trade. Albert and Viktor, father and son, were cutters in the fine traditional sense. Indeed, in their day nothing fundamental had changed in cutting since medieval times; stones were expected to look as they always had through the previous generations. There seemed no need to change. Viktor's son, Bernd, began by following the family in the traditions of cutting and carried out his apprenticeship from 1957 to 1962, learning all the traditional gem-cutting techniques that would later enable him to develop his own

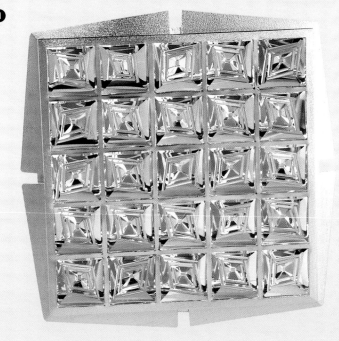

style. He decided to continue his studies as a gem cutter by exploring design, and from 1962 to 1966 attended the newly created class for "The Design of Precious Stones" at the School of Arts and Crafts in Pforzheim. His tutors, Professors Schollmeyer and Ullrich, together with goldsmith Erich Frey, encouraged his desire to, as Bernd put it, "do something different, something extraordinary". His studies encompassed all areas of design, including graphics, so it was some time before he actually cut stones again. His studies of gemmology, however, led him to become fascinated by internal reflection, the way that light behaves when entering and leaving a stone, and this became his great passion and inspiration. While at Pforzheim, he studied alongside many other students who were to become famous for their jewellery, including the jeweller Robert Smit, qualifying as a designer of precious stones and jewellery in 1966.

Bernd returned home and immediately opened a gem-cutting studio. Since then his pieces, from the ones in

his first exhibition in Frankfurt in 1967 to those he is producing today, have won both admiration and many awards. Soon after the opening of his studio Bernd was visited by Andrew Grima, then the British crown jeweller, who bought four cut gems from him and ordered more. This was indeed a fine tribute to such a new cutter.

Unlike commercial gem cutters who follow strict parameters, Bernd Munsteiner begins either with a new idea or takes his lead from the particular piece of rough, uncut mineral that lies before him. Starting with a sketch, he considers both the tactile quality and the visual appearance of the stone. He then removes all unwanted material to reach a basic shape, and creates his unmistakably unique pieces using a combination of incision, saw cuts, bored holes or facets to provide the asymmetrical and geometric forms that are so different from the standard oval and round cuts, and far more exotic than the square or rectangular ones introduced at the beginning of the twentieth century. Even the humble agate is not only cut but the designs are emphasized by the "sand blasting" of some areas, using corundum grains to gain a smooth but textured surface. These styles, free from convention and tradition, are seemingly playful in design, but are actually carefully thought out to provide a purity and clarity of form, using optical laws to flood transparent stones with light as well as to refract it.

Bernd makes a trip to Brazil every year to personally select the finest and most unusual crystals including aquamarine, tourmaline, citrine, amethyst and the colourless quartz that is often riddled with interesting inclusions. When asked what it is that fascinates him about these stones he has said: "Their high refraction, their distinct colours,

their luminosity. Light is the element of life for human beings. The play of light in a free design is my inspiration. The investigation of the way the stones reflect light is what fascinates me."

1 A brooch pendant by Bernd Munsteiner using twenty-five morganites which total 43 carats, called "Morganite Reflection".
2 A 45-carat, blue tourmaline stone cut by Bernd Munsteiner.
3 Bernd (left) and Tom Munsteiner at the cutting wheel in their workshop.

❸

4

Like all lapidaries, he cuts only coloured gems and hardstones such as agate, not diamonds, but he has designed cuts for these most demanding stones. In the 1990s, he developed the "context cut", a refinement of the basic octahedral form of the perfect diamond crystal. This needs such a perfect crystal that only one in 100,000 is suitable. This principle of a cut with two points, one at the top and the other at the bottom, was further developed to create a round stone, with thirty-two rather than his original eight facets. Both cuts received top design awards in 1997 and 1998.

Bernd has continued to explore and expand, and has produced many series of named cuts for setting in jewellery – including "reflecting perspectives", "inside selecting", "erotica" and "symbolon", but finds that sculptures free him from the constraints of setting considerations. His most famous sculpture is the 10,363-carat obelisk of aquamarine named "Dom Pedro", the largest cut aquamarine of gem quality in the world. This was followed by the 830 kilogram (about 1,830 pound) monster crystal of rutilated quartz (quartz with an inclusion of rods of rutile that reflect the light like golden hair) that would be turned into the fabulous sculpture entitled "Metamorphose 1". Many of these fantastic works of art are now in well-known institutions and collections, including the headquarters of the Gemological Institute of America and museums throughout the world.

Bernd's work is pioneering, demonstrating creativity and imagination, and it shows a sensitivity for structure, composition and dimension. He has been said to instil a spirit into the cut gemstones that places them alongside fine paintings, books, music scores and other masterpieces of art, to the point that one journalist called him "the Picasso of precious stones".

He has freed the gem-cutting industry from its previous conservatism and enabled many cutters to follow his lead.

His sons Jorg and Tom Munsteiner continue the family work. Jorg became a jeweller, and attended the Idar Oberstein School of Design. After graduating in 1990, he immediately went to work for Andrew Grima, who was then in Switzerland, before opening his own business in 1992 as a goldsmith jeweller setting Munsteiner stones.

Younger brother Tom took over the Munsteiner Atelier in 1997 and, although greatly influenced by the works around him, has created his own style of cutting that is generally more understated than his father's frequently jagged cuts. He attended the same school of design as his brother and qualified in 1995. He then went on to pass the exams of the German Gemmological Institute. He shares his father's feel for colour and form, but his work is soft and organic rather than hard and angular. He cuts hemispherical recesses in the back of basic geometric-shaped stones such as circular or square ones, which produces interesting three-dimensional effects, and thus his cuts do not always follow the natural features of a stone. Tom has also won many awards for his exciting designs and continues to run the family business with great success.

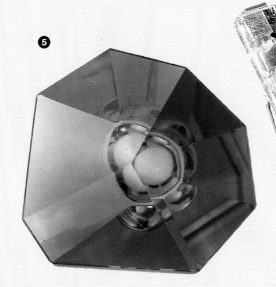

4 A large naturally coloured citrine of 178 carats cut by Bernd and mounted as a pendant, shown here with a stand that enables it to be viewed as a sculpture.
5 A citrine of 17 carats, cut by Tom Munsteiner.
6 This Munsteiner-cut quartz has been mounted by Jutta Munsteiner as a brooch pendant with thirteen natural pearls and is entitled "Onda".

Jutta, Tom's wife, is the family's other designer and sets Munsteiner masterpieces to provide highly individual works of jewellery. She believes that women do not want jewels to show what they have, but rather who they are, and thus rejects jewellery as a status symbol. Columbus' discovery of a new horizon was the inspiration of her creation "The Wave" – "to sail out to explore a promising, exciting new time".

All Munsteiner stones are engraved with their signature monogram or the full name, where possible, and all jewellery is signed. Stones are accompanied by a "passport" detailing the name, colour and carat weight of the stone, and these carry either Bernd's or Tom's signature, together with an image of the jewel.

Not only are these fabulous stones a representation of a massively important change in direction in gem cutting, but their immense historical and artistic importance is almost outweighed by their sheer beauty. These are important factors when considered individually, but taken as a whole must surely indicate superb value for money and a sound investment for the future.

COLLECTORS' INFORMATION

Introduction

Nearly everyone will buy a piece of jewellery at some point. It may be as a gift for a relative or friend, a treat for oneself, or to create an image at work. The cost involved can be great or small, from important purchases such as an engagement ring, through to a small piece of costume jewellery bought to accessorise a new outfit. The satisfaction gained from the ownership of a well-chosen piece of jewellery such as a fashionable necklace or a pair of smart cufflinks can be expanded to encompass the joy of collecting. There is a wealth of variety stemming from the jewels created in the twentieth century, and these alone can form a strong and varied collection. It could be formed around a particular style such as Art Deco or Retro, a type of jewellery such as Art or Contemporary, a favourite gem stone or maker, or cover the entire spectrum of the century. The latter may be achieved at a smaller cost by collecting costume jewellery, which usually follows fashions in precious jewels quite closely but can also provide opportunities for collectors in its own right. The act of buying jewellery can be fraught with problems, and the following section aims to provide information for both established collectors and those with a passing interest, offering guidelines to help start a collection and practical advice to those just wishing to purchase interesting pieces of jewellery.

Collectors' tips

Forming a jewellery collection, like collecting in any field, can provide immense pleasure – and not only in the fun of the hunt, chase and eventual acquisition. Unlike most other collectables, jewellery has another side. It can be worn. This can shed a different light on why or what is purchased, what condition it should be in and how much you want to spend.

WHAT TO CHOOSE

Buy jewellery for pleasure rather than sheer investment. The status and enjoyment you acquire by wearing it represents the interest on your capital. If you have bought wisely, and are lucky, you may be able to realize a financial profit as well as enjoying the fun of wearing your jewellery, but if the market is not kind and the value of what you have bought decreases you will still own something you like. When considering the purchase of a particular piece, always try it on and imagine how easy (or not) it will be to wear. Remember, sharp edges and points will snag clothes and high settings on rings will be easily knocked and damaged. Also be aware of the size of what you are buying. For most single-stone rings, altering the finger size will be inexpensive and easily done, but more complicated settings may be difficult - for example, it is impossible to resize an eternity ring without rebuilding it entirely. Similar considerations should be borne in mind with plain and hinged bangles. It may not be possible to enlarge short bracelets unless they are of a design that can accommodate additional links, and this is especially important for watches with integral rather than separate bracelets.

As with most things, it is wise to buy the best you can afford, so always examine jewellery on the back as well as the front. Here you will see the quality of finish and standard of workmanship, the pins and fittings, signature and any hallmarks or registrations.

CONDITION AND RELIABILITY

When examining the front and back of your prospective purchase, check for any lead (soft) solder repairs. These are usually fairly apparent and look like messy grey areas, either thick or thin, around new pins, catches, splits, joins and other repairs. Avoid pieces with these repairs if at all possible. The solder will corrode the alloys that make up gold and silver, and any effective repair to replace it will be difficult and costly, if not impossible. If you want a particular piece that has suffered badly over the years, it should be priced accordingly. A good example will still be worth having at the right price and you may be able to upgrade later.

Buy from an established and trusted source, remembering that gold, diamonds and coloured gems have hard-to-detect simulants. Also remember that the style and period of a piece, as well as its materials, can be of a dubious nature. There have been many revivalist periods when popular styles were reintroduced and few of these have remained uncopied. But can you tell the difference between the real thing and a copy? Not all copies are fakes meant to deceive – some are "tribute pieces", but these may not be brand-new either and so may fall into their own area of collecting.

The maker's name or signature may also be spurious. Again, sometimes it is a complete copy, whilst in other cases a recently engraved name may have been added to a period piece of good quality in an effort to further improve its value. Trusting the vendor, proprietor or your adviser is very important. You must feel that, should you later realize that there is a problem, you can return the piece without having a major battle on your hands.

OTHER ASPECTS

If an item has an interesting provenance, be sure that any documents, photographs and associated material remain with the jewel, or can easily be identified as purporting to it. Not only does this give added interest to your collection but it will very probably add value to the piece. Remember that several countries forbid the importation of products such as ivory and tortoiseshell regardless of age. The fact that an animal died nearly a hundred years ago is no longer acceptable, so when travelling be aware of what you are wearing or taking with you.

Lastly, take advantage of the opportunity to handle as much jewellery as you can. This can be done very effectively at auctions. The major auction houses are all very happy to advise on estimates and conditions, and their past catalogues can provide useful references.

Christie's addresses

AMSTERDAM

1071 JG Amsterdam
Tel: 31 (0) 20 57 55 255

EDINBURGH

5 Wemyss Place
Edinburgh EH3 6DH
Tel: 44 (0) 131 225 4756

GENEVA

8 Place de la Taconnerie
1204 Geneva
Tel: 41 (0) 22 319 17 66

HONG KONG

2203-5 Alexandra House
16-20 Chater Road
Hong Kong Central
Tel: 852 2521 5396

LONDON

8 King Street
St James's
London SW1Y 6QT
Tel: 44 (0) 20 7839 9060

LONDON

85 Old Brompton Road
London SW7 3LD
Tel: 44 (0) 20 7581 7611

LOS ANGELES

360 North Camden Drive
Beverly Hills
CA 90210
Tel: 1 310 385 2600

MELBOURNE

1 Darling Street
South Yarra, Melbourne
Victoria 3141
Tel: 61 (0) 3 9820 4311

MILAN

1 Piazza Santa Maria delle Grazie
20123 Milan
Tel: 39 02 467 0141

MONACO

Park Palace
98000 Monte Carlo
Tel: 377 97 97 11 00

NEW YORK

20 Rockefeller Plaza
New York
NY 10020
Tel: 1 212 636 2000

ROME

Palazzo Massimo Lancellotti
Piazza Navona 114
00186 Rome
Tel: 39 06 686 3333

SINGAPORE

Unit 3, Parklane
Goodwood Park Hotel
22 Scotts Road
Singapore 228221
Tel: 65 235 3828

TAIPEI

13F, Suite 302, No. 207
Tun Hua South Road
Section 2
Taipei 106
Tel: 886 2 2736 3356

TEL AVIV

4 Weizmann Street
Tel Aviv 64239
Tel: 972 (0) 3 695 0695

ZURICH

Steinwiesplatz
8032 Zurich
Tel: 41 (0) 1 268 1010

Museum addresses

EUROPE

MUSEE DU LOUVRE

75058 Paris Cedex 01
Tel: (33) 01 40 20 50 50
E-mail: info@louvre.fr
www.louvre.fr

MUSEE DES ARTS DECORATIFS

107 Rue de Rivoli
75001 Paris
Tel: 44 55 57 50
www.paris.org/Musees/Deoratifs

MUSEE D'ORSAY

62 Rue de Lille
75343 Paris
Tel: 33 (0)1 40 49 48 14
www.musee-orsay.fr

DEUTSCHES EDELSTEINMUSEUM

Haupstrasse 118
D-55743 Idar-Oberstein
Tel: (+49) 06781-90 09 80
E-mail: info@edelsteinmuseum.de
www.edelsteinmuseum.de

MUSEUM FUR KUNST UND GEWERBE

Steintorplatz 1
D-20099 Hamburg
Tel: 040 42854 2630
E-mail: service@mkg-hamburg.de
www.mkg-hamburg.de

SCHMUCKMUSEUM PFORZHEIM

Jahnstrasse 42
75173 Pforzheim
Tel: 07231 39 2126
E-mail: neish@stadt-pforzheim.de
www.schmuckmuseum-pforzheim.de

THE BRITISH MUSEUM

Great Russell Street
London WC1B 3DG
Tel: (+44) 020 7323 8299
E-mail: information@thebritish
    museum.ac.uk
www.thebritishmuseum.ac.uk

THE GOLDSMITH'S COMPANY

Goldsmith's Hall
Foster Lane
London EC2V 6BN
Tel: +44 (0) 20 7606 7010
www.thegoldsmiths.co.uk

THE VICTORIA AND ALBERT MUSEUM

Cromwell Road
South Kensington
London SW7 2RL
Tel: +44 (0) 20 7942 2000
E-mail: vanda@vam.ac.uk
www.vam.ac.uk

USA

METROPOLITAN MUSEUM OF ART

1000 Fifth Avenue
New York NY 10028
Tel: 212 535 7710
www.metmuseum.org

AMERICAN MUSEUM OF NATURAL HISTORY

Central Park West at 79th Street
New York   NY 10024
Tel: 212 769 5000
www.amnh.org

THE SMITHSONIAN INSTITUTION

Smithsonian Information
SI Building Room 153
Washington DC 20560
Tel: 202 357 2700
E-mail: info@si.edu
www.si.edu

Glossary

Acrylic – Plastic resin used for Contemporary Jewellery since the 1960s. Capable of being moulded and cut, it is available in a wide colour range.

Agate – Microcrystalline variety of chalcedony quartz, with distinct bands of varied colours.

Aigrette – Vertical ornament rising from the forehead, usually in the form of a plume of egret feathers.

Baguette – Term used for diamonds and gems of narrow rectangular cut. From the French word for "rod".

Baroque pearl – Pearl of irregular shape. May be induced in cultured pearls by the use of a misshaped nucleus.

Blister pearl – Pearl that was attached to the inner shell of the mollusc while it grew; may be hollow.

Bourse – Exchange where merchants in a specific material transact business.

Brilliant cut – Normal style of cutting for round diamonds, with fifty-eight facets to achieve maximum reflection.

Briolette-cut – Pear- or drop-shaped stone, usually diamond, of circular cross-section, the surface entirely covered with triangular facets.

Buff-top – Gem with a smooth polished crown and faceted pavilion.

Calibrated – Stones cut to standardized sizes for use in cast mounts produced in quantity.

Calibré – Style of cutting small gemstones into required shapes, often oblong or elliptical, to fit a design.

Cameo – Manner of carving in which the subject stands proud of the background. Any material may be used but the most frequent are banded agate and conch shell.

Claw setting – Common method of securing a gem by grasping the girdle with a series of encircling projecting prongs.

Cloisonné enamel – Enamel made by building up cloisons or cells with metal strips soldered to the surface to be decorated and filling them with enamel.

Conchiolin – Organic substance secreted by molluscs that binds the aragonite crystals that form a pearl.

Corsage – Spray worn on the bodice of a woman's dress.

Creole – A design inspired by traditional jewellery of the early French settlers in Louisiana, USA.

Crown – The portion above the girdle of any faceted gemstone.

Demantoid Garnet – A brilliant green garnet coloured by traces of chromium. Discovered in Russia in 1868 and from a new source in Namibia in 1998.

Diadem – Ornamental band worn around the brow, developed from ancient wreaths.

Drusy – Mass of tiny scintillating crystals still attached to their rock matrix, used in their natural form.

Enamel – Powdered glass, coloured with metallic oxides and bound with oil, which fuses when fired in a kiln.

En tremblant – Parts of large jewels, often flower sprays, mounted on tiny springs so that they quiver or tremble in wear.

Fancy (colour) – Term used on certificates for diamonds of an unusual natural colour.

Giardinetto – Literally "small garden"; usually rings or brooches set with varicoloured gems modelled as a bouquet or vase of flowers.

Girdle – Thin band that forms the widest circumference of a brilliant and separates the crown above from the pavilion below.

Guilloche enamel – Thin film of translucent enamel applied over lathe-cut engine-turned decoration.

Hardstone – Any decorative opaque stone, usually of small value.

Inclusion – Any visible internal crystal, growth structure or fracture in the body of a gemstone.

Intaglio – Form of carving where a design is cut into the surface of a gem or hardstone, sometimes as a mirror image for use as a seal.

Jabot pin – Used to secure the jabot, a ruffle worn on the front of a dress or shirt.

Lavallière (*or lavalier*) – Flexible neck chain or strand of beads from which one or more gemstones is suspended. The name is probably derived from Louise de la Vallière, mistress of Louis XIV of France.

Mabé pearl – A cultured blister pearl formed around a nucleus glued to the inside of the oyster shell. On recovery the attachment area is ground down and covered with a mother-of-pearl disc.

Matrix – Natural rock within, or on which, a crystal or gem material has developed.

Minaudière – Lady's composite accessory incorporating cigarette case, lighter, comb, cosmetics and mirror in one case.

Mosaic – Decoration made by arranging many small pieces (tesserae) of inlaid varicoloured glass or stone to form a picture or design.

Nucleus – Bead, normally formed from mother-of-pearl, inserted into the mantle of an oyster as the basis for the formation of a cultured pearl.

Parure – A suite of matching gem-set jewellery including necklace, bracelets, brooch, ring, earrings and hair ornament. A partial suite is termed demi-parure.

Paste – Glass used to resemble gemstones, usually containing lead oxide.

Pavé-set – Numerous small diamonds or gems set as closely together as possible, with minimal setting visible.

Pavilion – The part of a diamond or gem below the girdle.

Piqué – Term used in diamond grading for a stone with numerous inclusions.

Plique-à-jour – Translucent enamel in a frame with no backing so that light passes through the enamel to create an effect similar to stained glass.

Prismatic colours – The seven colours of the rainbow into which white light is split when it passes through facets that are at particular angles to each other.

Reflection – Returning or rebounding of light rays that strike a surface. The angle of reflection is equal to the angle of incidence.

Refraction – Bending of light rays as they pass from one medium, for example air, to another medium of different optical density, for example a gemstone.

Rub-over – Setting in which the edge of the mount is bent (rubbed) over the girdle in a continuous band.

Sautoir – Long necklace or chain worn loosely from the shoulders and often extending below the waist; often with tassel terminals.

Stomacher – A large piece of jewellery worn between the decolletage and the waist, sometimes articulated.

Tank – Style of rectangular wristwatch, the outline of which is based on the shape of the World War One armoured tank.

Torc – Metal neck ring or armlet formed as an open hoop, usually with ornamental terminals, derived from Celtic originals.

Tubogas – Form of gold necklace or bracelet; sprung metal is wound in a continuous coil inspired by flexible gas piping.

Tutti-frutti – Art Deco jewellery of the 1930s set with a "Fruit Salad" colour range of gems carved and modelled as flowers, berries and leaves.

Bibliography

BOOKS

Arwas, Victor, *Art Deco*, Academy Editions, London 1980

Bainbridge, Henry Charles, *Peter Carl Fabergé*, Spring Books, London 1949

Balfour, Ian, *Famous Diamonds*, Christie's Books, London 2000

Banham, Mary and Hillier, Bevis (editors), *A Tonic to the Nation*, Thames and Hudson, London 1976

Becker, Vivienne, *Art Nouveau Jewellery*, Thames and Hudson, London 1985

Becker, Vivienne, *The Jewellery of René Lalique*, The Goldsmiths Company, London 1987

Bennett, David and Mascetti, Daniela, *Understanding Jewellery*, Antique Collectors' Club, Suffolk, England 1989

Bury, Shirley, *Jewellery, The International Era 1789-1910*, Antique Collectors' Club, Suffolk, England 1991

Cailles, Françoise, *René Boivin Jeweller*, Quartet Books, London, 1994

Drucker, Janet, *Georg Jensen A Tradition of Splendid Silver*, Schiffer Publishing, Pennsylvania, USA 1997

Dubbs Ball, Joanne, *Costume Jewelers The Golden Age of Design*, Schiffer Publishing, Pennsylvania, USA 1990

Farnetta Cera, Deanna (editor), *Jewels of Fantasy Costume Jewelry of the 20th Century*, Harry N. Abrams, New York 1992

Gaal, Robert A. P., Ph.D., *The Diamond Dictionary (second edition)*, Gemological Institute of America, Santa Monica, USA 1977

Gere Charlotte and Culme, John, *Garrard, The Crown Jewellers for 150 Years*, Quartet Books, London 1993

Jaquet, Eugène and Chapuis, Alfred, *Technique and History of the Swiss Watch*, Hamlyn Publishing, London 1970

Lewin, Susan Grant, *American Art Jewelry Today*, Thames and Hudson, London 1994

Loring, John, *Paulding Farnham, Tiffany's Lost Genius*, Harry N. Abrams, New York 2000

Loring, John, *Tiffany Jewels*, Harry N. Abrams, New York 1999

Menkes, Suzy, *The Royal Jewels*, Grafton Books, London 1985

Muller, Andy, *Cultured Pearls, The First Hundred Years*, Golay Buchel Group, Lausanne, Switzerland 1997

Nadelhoffer, Hans, *Cartier Jewellers Extraordinary*, Thames and Hudson, London 1984

Neret, Gilles, *Boucheron Four Generations of a World-Renowned Jeweler*, Rizzoli International Publications, New York 1988

Newman, Harold, *An Illustrated Dictionary of Jewelry*, Thames and Hudson, London 1981

Parry, Linda (editor), *William Morris*, Philip Wilson Publishers in Association with the Victoria and Albert Museum, London 1996

Pullee, Caroline, *20th Century Jewellery*, Grange Books, London 1997

Raulet, Sylvie, *Jewellery of the 1940s and 1950s*, Thames and Hudson, London 1988

Rudoe, Judy, *Cartier 1900-1939*, British Museum Press, London 1997

Scarisbrick, Diana (consultant editor), *Jewellery, Makers, Motifs, History, Techniques*, Thames and Hudson, London 1989

Snowman, Kenneth (editor), *The Master Jewellers*, Thames and Hudson, London 1990

Watkins, David, *The Best in Contemporary Jewellery*, Quarto Publishing, London 1993

Watson, Linda, *Vogue, Twentieth Century Fashion*, Carlton, London 1999

Wietler, Dr Haidrun, *Munsteiner's Zeit*, Publicaciones Joyeras, Barcelona, Spain 2000

Zapata, Janet, *The Jewellery and Enamels of Louis Comfort Tiffany*, Harry N. Abrams, New York 1993

MAGAZINES

The Basel Magazine, CRU Publishing Ltd

The Retail Jeweller, Tower Publishing Services

Diamonds - the four Cs

Used to convey the information that dictates the value of a diamond, the four Cs are Cut, Colour, Clarity and Carat weight. The most often quoted and internationally accepted scale is set by the GIA, the Gemological Institute of America, and will be used in certificates issued by renowned laboratories following grading by professionals. See page 120 for more information on diamonds.

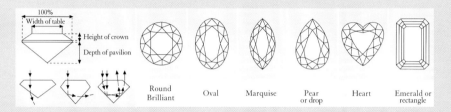

CUT This will describe the shape of the stone and determine the quality of the cutting together with a judgement on how good the proportions are for that particular cut.

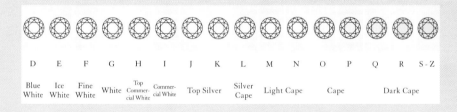

COLOUR Graded from D, totally without colour, descending alphabetically, H is where the first hint of yellow can be seen, as the scale progresses the tints become stronger. Traditional terminology is shown beneath the GIA grades.

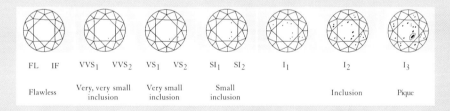

CLARITY The number, size and colour of inclusions, when viewed under 10x magnification in normal daylight or the equivalent. From flawless to very spotty *piqué* at the bottom of the scale.

0.01 carat	0.02 carat	0.03 carat	0.05 carat	0.10 carat	0.15 carat	0.20 carat	0.25 carat
1.35 mm	1.70 mm	2.00 mm	2.40 mm	3.00 mm	3.40 mm	3.80 mm	4.10 mm
0.30 carat	0.40 carat	0.50 carat	0.75 carat	1.00 carat	2.00 carat	3.00 carat	4.00 carat
4.40 mm	4.70 mm	5.00 mm	5.80 mm	6.50 mm	8.20 mm	9.50 mm	10.50 mm

CARAT The size of a stone is usually indicated by the carat weight. The modern brilliant is cut to a mathematical standard so that size and weight will be directly comparable. Therefore the use of a gauge with holes set at these diameters indicates the weight of a diamond that fits, or measurements taken compared to set tables.

Index

A

Academy Awards Ceremonies 157

acrylics in jewellery design 119

African art, and Art Deco 55–6

Aga Kahn, Princess Nina 77, 85

Aletto Brothers 140

Alexandra, Queen 39, 41

Algae jewellery 99

Allan, Susan 135, 136

amber 16, 155–6, 157

antique jewellery 106–8

Antiques Roadshow 31, 34

Art Deco 17–18, 42, 48–63, 82

 in the 1930s 60–2

 and African art 55–6

 baguette cut diamonds 51, 121

 colours 56, 60–1

 costume jewellery 143

 cutting styles 56

 and the Darmstadt colony 50

 Di Portanova collection 151

 dress clips 17, 141

 Egyptian motifs in 55, 56, 168

 exhibitions 50–1

 Indian motifs in 56

 and Indo-Persian styles 56

 jungle theme 57–8

 ladies' accessories 56–8

 and ladies' fashions 51–2

 and the modernist movement 54–5

 revivals 110, 169

 watches 52–4

Art Nouveau 10–12, 12–13, 15, 26–31, 32, 38, 42, 50

 in the 1970s 110

 commercialization and mechanization of 30–1

 and German Jugendstil design 11, 30

 and Japanese design 10–11, 26, 28, 29

 materials 26

 necklaces 18–19, 26, 28, 31

 publications 28

 revival 169

 sensuality in 26, 27, 28

 and World War Two 70

Artificers' Guild silver and gem necklace 34

Artist Jewellers 119, 132, 135–9, 141

Arts and Crafts movement 11, 12, 30, 31–8, 42, 70

 art guilds 34–6

 independent designers 32–4

 revival 169

Ashbee, C.R. 32, 34–5

Austria, Wiener Werkstatte 35, 36

Austrian Association of Applied Artists 35–6

B

Baker, Josephine 56

Bakker, Gijs 114, 139

Bakst, Leon 55

Baldaccini, César 136

ballerina brooches 73

bandeaux 40, 52

bangles

 Cartier love bangles 158

 Chimaera 82–4

 jade and diamond 171

 Perspex 119

 street fashion 104

 Verdura 84, 86

Barbier, George 57

Basha, Aaran 161–2

Bauhaus movement 17, 54

Becker, Friedrich 119

Behrens, Peter 30, 50

Belperron, Suzanne 77, 79

Bennett, James 115

Bernhardt, Sarah 26, 28

Biba 108–10

Bing, Marcel 29

Bing, Samuel 11, 26, 29, 36

Binns, Tom 108

black diamonds 158, 159

black pearl necklace 107, 108

body-piercing jewellery 154

Boivin, Olivier 19

Boivin, René 99

Bombay Trading Co. 56

Bosselt, Rudolph 36, 50

Boston Society of Arts and Crafts 35

Boucheron, Frédéric 14, 29, 39, 56

Boucheron, Louis 58–60, 62, 81, 82

Bouquin, Jean 98

Bozzachi, Louis 85

bracelet-watches 82, 106

bracelets

 Art Deco 52, 55, 58, 59, 60, 62, 168

 costume jewellery 140

 Garland Style 43

 gold and diamond 158

 Massoni 151

 power bracelets 155

 Retro 72, 82, 83, 87, 168

 street fashion 102

Braque, Georges 89

Britain

 Arts and Crafts movement 12, 32–5, 36

 Festival of (1951) 90

 hallmarking system 165–6

 jewellery trade in the 1950s 90

 mourning jewellery in 14

 Roman invasion of 44

 see also London

Broadhead, Caroline 119

Dedication

To Jane Everitt and Sidney Lancaster.

Acknowledgements

Stephen Kennedy and the Gem Testing Laboratory of Great Britain for images of pearl and cultured pearl x-rays, and synthetic ruby structure.
Bernd and Tom Munsteiner for pictures of their work.
Andy Johnson and Alberto Gonzales for their photography at Christie's South Kensington.
Emma Strouts, Edward Elphick and Margarita Crutchley from Christie's Images.